"[This] isn't a book of Great Truths. It's just Lewis sitting behind his 1959 Royal manual typewriter in Atlanta telling us what he sees—a lot of little truths. Some of the columns are funny, some are nostalgic and some make you think deep (well, semi-deep anyway) thoughts.... Think of it as reality therapy."

Colorado Springs Gazette Telegraph

"A collection of his funniest most outrageous columns yet."

Orangeburg Times Democrat

"Of all his books, I believe this one is the funniest....Outrageous...Grizzard tears up our existing technological age with humor as he considers computers, answering machines and hair dryers. ...This is a funny book, and don't you need a laugh or two about this time of year?"

Jacksonville Daily News

Also by Lewis Grizzard:

Books
DON'T BEND OVER IN THE GARDEN, GRANNY,
 YOU KNOW THEM TATERS GOT EYES*
MY DADDY WAS A PISTOL AND I'M A SON OF A
 GUN
SHOOT LOW, BOYS—THEY'RE RIDIN' SHETLAND
 PONIES*
ELVIS IS DEAD AND I DON'T FEEL SO GOOD
 MYSELF
IF LOVE WERE OIL, I'D BE ABOUT A QUART LOW
THEY TORE OUT MY HEART AND STOMPED THAT
 SUCKER FLAT
DON'T SIT UNDER THE GRITS TREE WITH
 ANYONE ELSE BUT ME
WON'T YOU COME HOME, BILLY BOB BAILEY?
KATHY SUE LOUDERMILK, I LOVE YOU
CHILI DAWGS ALWAYS BARK AT NIGHT*
IF I EVER GET BACK TO GEORGIA, I'M GONNA
 NAIL MY FEET TO THE GROUND*
YOU CAN'T PUT NO BOOGIE-WOOGIE ON THE
 KING OF ROCK AND ROLL*
I HAVEN'T UNDERSTOOD ANYTHING SINCE 1962

Comedy Albums
ON THE ROAD WITH LEWIS GRIZZARD
LEWIS GRIZZARD LIVE
LET'S HAVE A PARTY WITH LEWIS GRIZZARD

*Published by Ballantine Books

When My Love Returns From The Ladies Room, Will I Be Too Old To Care?

Lewis Grizzard

BALLANTINE BOOKS • NEW YORK

Copyright © 1987 by Lewis Grizzard

All rights reserved under International and Pan-American Copyright Conventions. Published in the United States of America by Ballantine Books, a division of Random House, Inc., New York, and simultaneously in Canada by Random House of Canada Limited, Toronto.

Library of Congress Catalog Card Number: 87-40183

ISBN 0-345-35785-X

This edition published by arrangement with Villard Books, a division of Random House, Inc.

Manufactured in the United States of America

First Ballantine Books Edition: January 1989
Tenth Printing: August 1993

**To Gerrie,
for all you do**

Contents

CONTENTS

Introduction

I have just completed ten years of writing a newspaper column. The first year, I wrote six a week. After a year, I whined enough to my superiors to get that cut to five. Five years ago, I went to four. I figure another fifteen or twenty years, I won't have to write any columns whatsoever, but by that time, I'll probably be senile and saying the same things I've said before over and over again and nobody will want to read what I write anyway, and I'll probably have trouble going to the bathroom, too.

Since this is the tenth anniversary of my column, I thought I would do a number of things here, in this introduction, including telling how I came to be a newspaper columnist in the first place:

The deal on the liquor store fell through.

I also thought I would answer some of the many questions people have asked me over the years about what I do for a living. Here goes:

1. Why do you drink so much?

It makes it easier to forgive myself for getting into this line of work. I could have gone to law school, or, better yet, been a chiropractor. If I hadn't been such an honest person when I was younger, I probably would have done one of the above. Today, I could be doing my own television commercials and be a member of an Elks club.

Instead, I go around making a living insulting perfectly fine institutions like the Elks club.

2. Where do you get your daily ideas?

I belong to an idea service. I pay $38.50 twice annually, and a firm in Oregon sends me an idea for a column four times a week. For $50 twice annually, I could get good ideas, but I decided to save my money like the television networks do when they order programming ideas.

3. Have you ever been arrested?

It was when I was in high school. I was picked up for mooning another car, but I was released when they found out it was my head I had stuck out the window.

4. Do you ever get writer's block?

As a matter of fact, I feel a bad case of it coming on now.

5. How much do you make?

6. Have you ever had sex with anybody famous?

7. Do you trim your toenails regularly?

8. What is the capital of South Dakota?

9. Why did the army turn you down?

10. Can you explain why, if you're such a hot stuff writer, you've never won any big awards like the Pulitzer Prize, been on the cover of *Time* magazine, met Russell Baker, had a drink at Elaine's in New York, been on *The Oprah Winfrey Show,* appeared at halftime of an NFL game, or died at Joanna Carson's house?

I think the writer's block attack has passed, so we can go on.

There have been many great lines about writing a column. Unfortunately, I've never had one, but I know some by other people, none of whom I am going to give credit.

—Writing a daily newspaper column is like being married to a nymphomaniac. The first two weeks, it's fun.

—The daily columnist's prayer: Lord, grant me my daily idea, and forgive me for yesterday's.

—Imagine Johnny Carson's monologue five nights a week without writers. That's what writing a newspaper column is about.

—Writing a column is easy. Just sit down at the typewriter and wait for the blood to pop out of your forehead.

But don't get the idea that writing a column is all fun. Sometimes, it is very difficult work, like the time I interviewed Fonda Love, a nude dancer (they used to call them "strippers") in a joint in Fort Lauderdale, Florida. The bouncer, a large gentleman who had no neck, made me put both hands behind my back while I interviewed Fonda Love. Ever try to take notes holding the pencil in your mouth?

Another time, I was assigned to write a column about a Club Med on Paradise Island in Nassau. The third day I was there, I saw a cloud.

There also are some risks involved in writing a newspaper column. Before my newspaper made everybody write on computers (everybody but me, this is coming to you by virtue of a 1959 Royal manual), they made us write on electric typewriters with those little balls that have all the letters and numbers and symbols on them.

One day, I was looking inside my electric typewriter to see from whence a rather strange sound was originating (the sound was sort of like two pigeons making love on a sheet of aluminum foil), and I got my shirt collar caught in the typewriter's works and was nearly typed to death by an out-of-control ampersand.

Also, people have written and once threatened to kill me because they said I wasn't a Christian, and I once wound up on the mailing list for a number of gay publications after I wrote a gay joke in my column: Did you hear about the two gay men who attacked a woman? One held her down while the other did her hair.

I've learned a great deal in my ten years of writing columns. Here are some of the things I have learned:

—At least five people will threaten to kill you if you mention anything that remotely has to do with God.

—There are a lot more gay publications than I ever had imagined.

—The slightest criticism of anybody who is black automatically makes you a racist.

—The women's movement is in serious need of a sense of humor.

—You eventually will come to realize that there is no subject about which you will not write a column. I have written about the hair that is growing in my ears, my shoes, mustard, goats and pigs, who to pull for in the Iran-Iraq war, and how good I thought *USA Today* is. My newspaper refused to run that last column.

—If it weren't for my assistant, Gerrie Ferris, I'd go crazy. I have dedicated this book to Gerrie and intend to let her have her own, autographed copy at an unbelievable discount price.

This brings me to a brief discussion about my books. This is my tenth anniversary of writing columns, and this is my tenth book. There is order to the universe after all.

The question most people ask me is, "How do you come up with the titles for your books?"

I did "Kathy Sue Loudermilk, I Love You," "Won't You Come Home, Billy Bob Bailey?," "Don't Sit Under the Grits Tree with Anybody Else but Me," and "Glory! Glory!" while suffering from terrible hangovers. (By the way, you may notice that my publisher lists only eight previous books. That's because they insist on leaving out *Glory! Glory!* because I was only the coauthor.)

My stepbrother, Ludlow Porch of WSB radio in Atlanta and also an author, contributed "They Tore Out My Heart and Stomped That Sucker Flat," and "If Love Were Oil, I'd Be About a Quart Low." I didn't pay him either time.

His former news editor at another radio station contributed, "My Daddy Was a Pistol and I'm a Sun of a Gun," which is a line from Roger Miller's song "Dang Me." We had to pay somebody in order to use that.

I also named "Elvis Is Dead and I Don't Feel So Good Myself." That came from the fact that a man who helped raise me, Mr. Bob Jenkins of Grantville, Georgia, retired from the post office and then sat around drinking Ancient Age and Coke and enjoying life, and he was all the time saying, "All great men are dying, and I don't feel so good myself."

I think it was Mark Twain who first said that, but, regardless, the line stuck in my mind and that's where "Elvis" came from.

One afternoon, Mr. Bob Jenkins's son, Ronnie, and I were drinking beer in Lucille Drake's beer joint near East Body Shop in Grantville and out of the blue, he said, "Shoot low, boys, they're ridin' shetland ponies," which, twenty years later, I used as a title for another book.

After this book was published, somebody told me the line came from an old western movie, but all I knew is I heard it from Ronnie Jenkins. I never paid him, either.

Now, to the title of this book, "When My Love Returns

from the Ladies Room, Will I Be Too Old to Care?"

That's mine, too. All I want to know is what do women do in the rest room for so long, and why do they always go in pairs?

What do they have in the ladies room that occupies so much of the visitor's time? Dress shops? Male strippers? Hairdressers named "Raoul" and "Dante?"

I've spent what seems like half my life waiting for some woman to come out of the ladies room. Some never came out. They apparently started new lives for themselves in there. Or, the suction was so great in the toilets, they were sucked down to the sewer and eaten by alligators.

Anyway, the title of this book is "When My Love Returns from the Ladies Room, Will I Be Too Old to Care?" and it's got sort of a ring to it, much more so than the original title, which was "I Hope You Get Sucked down the Toilet into the Sewer and Eaten by an Alligator."

Now, what I want you to do after you read this book is call all your friends and relatives and suggest—no, demand—they buy one, too.

None of this, "When I get through reading it, I'll lend it to you." If you happen to be in the real estate business, would you like to sell one house and then have everybody in town move into it?

Of course not. You want to see everybody buy their own house so you can make lots of money and be able to afford expensive stuff like ice cream with foreign-sounding names and trips to islands.

It's the same when you write a book. Everybody ought to have their own, personal book. I like expensive, foreign-made ice creams and trips to islands, too, as long as they aren't Three Mile or Rhode. I went to Rhode Island once, and it was very cold and none of the native women went around without their tops on. I can think of no reason to go back.

If that is not reason enough to try to gets lots of people to buy this book, here is another: God has told me if I don't sell at least two hundred fifty thousand of these books by February 1, it's curtains for me, which brings up the question, if Oral Roberts is such a godly person, why does he have a bad word for a first name?

And that brings up another question: Does Yasir Arafat have a brother named Nosir?

We will leave all that to ponder at another time.

In closing, I am currently hard at work on my eleventh book, which may or may not be the definitive volume on sex in America.

Please continue, and I hope you enjoy.

WOMEN

✳✳✳

Women Wearing Ties

I SAW A WOMAN ON AN AIRPLANE THE OTHER DAY WHO was wearing a tie. I don't think I had ever seen a woman wearing a tie before.

I thought only men wore ties to make up for the fact we don't have to get pregnant.

The woman in the tie looked like one of those big-time business women who owns her own condo, a BMW and a fluffy cat.

"Excuse me," I said to the woman. "I was just wondering why you are wearing a tie."

"Why not?" the woman asked me back.

"Well," I said, "I thought only men wore ties."

"You obviously are one of those Neanderthal redneck men who think women have no place in your world," said the woman, who was very irritated by my comment.

"Not at all, madam," I interrupted. "I certainly believe if a woman can do the same job as a man, she deserves the opportunity to do so and she should get the same pay as a man.

"The only thing I'm against women doing is voting and driving," I went on, in jest, of course.

I forgot, however, that the feminist movement is totally devoid of a sense of humor. I should have known the woman wouldn't take my little barb in the frivolous spirit in which it was intended.

Her eyes bugged out, her face turned red and the veins in her neck popped out in anger. She called me several unprintable names, a couple of which I have never heard before, leading me to believe women not only have equaled men in the ability to curse, but may have exceeded us.

I thought the woman was going to have a stroke, so I

3

suggested she loosen her tie. She did, and in a few minutes she seemed as calm as possible under the circumstances.

Upon some quiet reflection regarding this incident, I came to the conclusion that women certainly have a right to wear a tie anywhere at anytime.

In fact, I think it is only fair that all women be made to wear ties and men be allowed to stop the silly practice.

I quit wearing ties everywhere except to funerals of close friends several years ago when I decided I had had enough of being uncomfortable.

But I'm lucky. I don't have a real job like most men, so I can get away with not wearing a tie.

Ties are detrimental to men's health. Men who have to wear ties all the time tend to be high-strung and nervous because they've got this piece of cloth tied tightly around their necks. It's ties, not cholesterol, that cause most heart attacks and strokes.

Also, besides being terribly uncomfortable and unhealthy, it is a known fact that wearing a tie eventually leads to baldness. The tie hinders the circulation to the scalp and that's why men's hair falls out.

You don't see many baldheaded women, do you? Of course not. That's because they don't wear ties.

But it's high time they did. And it's high time men were relieved of this burden.

Imagine if the tie tables were turned and it was women who had to wear ties to get into a fancy restaurant. You walk in with your lady and she has forgotten her tie.

"You may enter, sir," the maitre d' would say, "but baldy there needs a tie."

What a simply delicious fantasy.

Shopping with a Woman

WHEN I SHOP FOR CLOTHING, I KEEP IT AS SIMPLE AS possible. I walk into a men's clothing store and say, "I would like to see some shirts, please."

The salesperson points me to the shirts, and I say, "I'll take this one and that one."

I'm out of there in less than five minutes. Life is too short to spend much of it fussing over new clothing.

Recently, it became my burden to accompany a young woman shopping. I won't bore you with the details of why I had to do this. Let us just say that no matter how hard a man tries to avoid going shopping with a woman, he eventually will be nailed.

It was a learning experience. I always thought women basically shopped like men. Not so. Women shop like they are on a mission from God.

"Banzai!" screamed the lady I was with when she entered the store.

What is this, I wondered? Samurai shopper?

The basic difference between male shoppers and female shoppers is that the latter group tries on everything in the store before they even come close to making a decision about a purchase.

I've bought houses in less time than it takes a woman to shop for a skirt and blouse.

I would like to see inside a dressing room in a woman's clothing shop. It must be bigger than a warehouse. The woman I was with took something from every rack in the place and then disappeared into the back with two salespersons and the stock boy, each of whom had their arms filled with apparel.

She was gone for a month, and then reappeared wearing a new outfit.

"How do you like this?" she asked.

What am I going to say? "You look like Omar the Tent-maker in that thing."

Of course not. Say something like that and she will be gone another month.

"I love it," I said of her outfit.

"You really like it, or are you just saying that so I will be finished shopping?"

Cunning devils, these people.

"No," I replied. "I swear I really like it. You remind me of Gina Lollobrigida in one of those biblical movies in that outfit."

That was the wrong thing to say.

"Gina Lollobrigida was a cow," she said tartly and disappeared back into the warehouse.

She must have tried on thirty more outfits. Each time, she asked my opinion. Each time, I said I thought she looked great, except for the time she came out in something that made her look like one of the Fruit of the Loom singers.

"Which one?" she asked.

"The banana, I think," I answered.

What else takes a long time when a woman shops is that with each outfit she tries on, she must also find matching shoes, belts, necklaces and earrings. It's like trying to put together one of those picture puzzles of Mount Rushmore that come in a thousand pieces.

We were there for an eternity before she finally came out and said, "Let's go."

"You're not going to buy anything?" I asked in disbelief.

"I didn't like a single thing," she said.

I went home and took two Midol. In a couple of hours, I was fine.

Women Drivers

DURING MY RECENT RECUPERATIVE PERIOD, I WAS NOT allowed to drive. Therefore, I had to elicit the help of others to drive me around to various appointments.

Once I even had a woman drive me.

I don't really have anything against women drivers, and statistics prove women actually are safer drivers than men.

However, there are certain facets of operating a motorized vehicle that women don't know beans about, and I seized the opportunity while having a woman drive me to attempt to teach at least one female person some of the finer points of motorized vehicling.

I must say this young woman was totally understanding about this learning experience.

"Why don't you just sit there and keep your mouth shut? I took driver's ed in high school," said my chauffeurette.

I knew, however, she was only kidding and was eager to learn, so I began with pulling up underneath an overhead signal light when waiting to turn left in traffic.

If a driver does not pull under a light when waiting to turn left in traffic and stays back behind the light, then the light will change back to red without anybody being able to turn left and motorists eventually will have to begin new lives for themselves in the line of traffic.

"Pull up all the way underneath the light and while it is changing back to red, you will be able to turn left," I coached my student.

"One more word out of you and you'll be back in the hospital," she said.

Next, we tackled parallel parking. Women cannot parallel park. They try, and, after failing, simply abandon their

7

cars half in and half out of the parking space.

"The key here," I said, "is to pull up even with the car in front of the parking place and then *back* into it."

"Why don't you back into a deep hole?" suggested the lady.

I also discussed using the proper lane while driving on an expressway. The main point I wanted to make was the left lane was the passing lane and should not be used as the lane in which to cruise at 11 miles per hour.

Often I am driving on an expressway, and I end up behind a woman who is cruising in the left lane at 11 miles per hour. These are the times I wish I had machine guns underneath my headlights.

I also went into such things as not applying eye shadow or combing hair while driving, not backing up on the expressway to catch a missed exit, and not stopping on a busy street to discuss Thursday's doubles match with a friend who is driving the other way.

I mentioned dimming lights when meeting an oncoming vehicle at night, not searching through a pocketbook for gum while driving over 30, not parking in fire lanes at shopping centers so as not to miss one minute of a shoe sale, and all the other things women do that are wrong when they drive.

When the lesson was over, I felt I had done at least something to promote better driving by our female friends.

"Women," I said to the taxi driver who took me home after I was put out on the street, helpless, "they don't appreciate anything."

"Zip it, creep, or I'll close that other eye," she said.

Women in the Men's Room

THE FABULOUS POINTER SISTERS APPEARED IN ATLANTA recently at an outdoor amphitheater, and there was much made over the fact that there were several drug busts during the performance.

I was at the concert, but it wasn't people putting illegal substances into their noses that bothered me.

What bothered me was what always bothers me when I attend a concert at this particular facility in Atlanta's Chastain Park, and that is women elbowing their way into the men's rest rooms.

I was at the Willie Nelson concert at Chastain. I had to go to the rest room. There were as many women in the men's room as men.

I was at the Anne Murray concert at Chastain. Same blasted thing.

The male reaction to this encroachment into what I consider one of the last bastions of male-only institutions was mixed.

Some of the men in the rest room apparently thought women joining them there was a hilarious happening. And they laughingly made crude remarks to the women, who seemed not to care as long as they had the opportunity to relieve themselves.

Other men, some of whom may have been putting illegal substances in their noses, appeared never to notice the phenomenon.

Others, including myself, got mad.

"Why don't you women go to your own rest room?" a

man shouted at the line of females awaiting their turn in the stalls.

"The line's too long in the women's room, that's why," one of the female spokespersons shot back.

There are two important points to be made here.

First, who is to blame that the line to any women's rest room always is longer than the one to the men's?

It's certainly not our fault, ladies. The reason the women's room line always is so long is that when a woman goes inside a rest room, she often takes the opportunity to do a complete overhaul on her face and hair and to talk about whatever it is women talk about when there are no men around.

I have known women who easily could spend an hour in a restaurant rest room and then come out and complain that their food is cold.

I've spent so much time waiting on women to come out of rest rooms, I once considered writing a love song titled "When My Love Returns from the Ladies Room, Will I Be Too Old to Care?"

The way to cut down on the lines to women's rest rooms is simple. Once a woman is inside she should take care of business as quickly as possible like the men do.

And point two: What would happen if men started going into women's rest rooms? I'll tell you what would happen. The National Organization for Women and other terrorist groups would scream and shout and turn red in the face and demand that such dastardly interlopers be beaten and jailed.

I have voiced my opinion on this matter before, because women have been infringing upon male privacy for some time now.

I believe, however, they are becoming more brazen in this practice, and if they don't stop, men might someday decide to retaliate and start crashing Tupperware parties.

Don't say you weren't warned, sisters.

Feminists Kidnap Grizzard

MR. ART HARRIS, ACE REPORTER FOR THE *WASHINGTON Post*, wrote an article about me recently, which indicates just how slow the news is in our nation's capital these days.

Mr. Harris even quoted one of my ex-wives. I thought she let me off easy by not telling him anything about some of my bad habits such as refusing to trim my toenails on the basis that you never know when you might have to climb a tree barefoot, at which time long toenails would come in handy.

However, one thing did disturb me about the article, and that was Mr. Harris's report that a group of feminists had plotted to kidnap me for some alleged show of sexism on my part.

After they kidnapped me, their plan was to tar and feather me in the middle of Atlanta.

Ladies, ladies, ladies. Aren't you going a little overboard here?

What have I done to make the feminists consider kidnapping, which is against the law, and tar-and-feathering, a favorite tactic of the Ku Klux Klan?

Have I ever said a woman should not make the same wages as a man if she could do the same job?

No.

Do I have a subscription to *Playboy* or *Penthouse* or other such publications that exploit women?

No, although when I was younger I did spend a lot of time browsing through the women's undergarment section of the Sears, Roebuck catalog, something I outgrew in my early twenties.

The truth is the feminists have me pegged all wrong.

I certainly am a man sensitive to the needs of modern

woman. I didn't even get angry in a bar recently when a woman standing next to me dropped an ash from her cigar and burned a hole in my jacket.

When I was sports editor in Chicago, I hired a female sportswriter, the first ever on the staff. I admit I assigned her to the soccer beat, but that's better than covering bowling.

I lost an arm-wrestling match to a woman once, and it did absolutely nothing to damage my ego, although my wrist was sore for a month. Cordie Mae Poovey, the girl who beat me, taught me early in life that certain women can outdo men in such physical endeavors as arm-wrestling, hair-pulling, belly-punching and shin-kicking.

I'm not certain Cordie Mae ever got involved in the feminist movement, but the fact she might have is another reason I refrain from overt acts of sexism. I don't want her to walk into my office one day and punch me in the belly and pull my hair and then kick me in the shins with her steel-toed brogans, as was her custom when angered in grade school.

I am glad the feminists called off their sinister plot against me, for whatever reasons, and I hope this column clears the air between us and will discourage them from any similar notions in the future.

And, if you don't want to shave your legs, my sisters, that's your business.

I've always felt the same way about trimming my toenails.

Miss Fribish Takes on Regan

YOU MUST KNOW BY NOW THAT WHITE HOUSE CHIEF OF Staff Donald Regan committed an unpardonable sin the other day by stating that women wouldn't understand the complicated issues of the Geneva summit.

This brought harsh reaction from leading feminists around the country including my personal secretary, the lovely and talented Miss Wanda Fribish.

Miss Fribish as well as being my personal secretary also is commandette of the 403rd Bombardier wing of the local chapter of the Fightin' Feminists.

She has been quite active in the fight for women's rights, claiming responsibility for the stink-bombing of three Jaycee meetings and two strip joints around the Atlanta area where women take off their clothes and are nothing more than sex objects for drooling men who go to those places.

Miss Fribish asked for a few days off in order to go to Washington so she could deal with Mr. Regan.

"I'll show that smart-mouthed pig who understands what!" explained Miss Fribish, resplendent in her camouflage outfit and designer combat boots.

Fortunately for Mr. Regan, however, Miss Fribish already had used all her days off during the recent Fightin' Feminists maneuvers which took place at a secret training site somewhere near Marietta, Georgia.

As most of my readers know, I am foresquare behind the women's movement, especially when Miss Fribish is standing over me and my typewriter with a pair of brass knuckles.

I must admit, however, that until the harsh reaction to Mr. Regan's remark, I didn't know that women not only could understand the complicated issues of the summit but actually would want to do so.

I must further admit that I, like a lot of other men, was under the mistaken illusion that women still dealt in what has been known as "girl talk."

Take a party, for instance. After everybody stands around with a drink in one hand and a sausage ball in the other, the men go in the den and the women go into the kitchen.

Men talk about sports, politics, the prime rate and occasionally tell humorous stories with a sexual angle.

Women gather in the kitchen. We thought they were talking about cute things their children said, recipes, fashion, upcoming Tupperware parties and neighborhood gossip.

Apparently we were wrong. Women were in the kitchen discussing complicated national and international issues.

"I'll tell you one thing, Madge," they apparently were saying, "if we don't get stringent verification methods, then I would say the arms talks were not worthwhile."

"I agree, Sylvia, but at least the meetings between Reagan and Gorbachev were cordial, but frank."

Donald Regan owes the women of this country an apology because they did understand the complicated issues of the Geneva summit.

Now I just hope they aren't so angry they won't do their male counterparts a big favor by explaining them to us.

Women's Caucus in Atlanta

THE SUMMER'S BIG EVENT IN ATLANTA OCCURRED RE-
cently when the National Women's Political Caucus came
to town.

For the first time America's top feminists, including
Gloria Steinem, astronautperson Sally Ride and Geraldine
Ferraro, came to the Deep South to hold one of their get-
togethers.

More than two thousand leaders of the women's movement were in the city, and my good friend Representative
Cathey Steinberg, one of Atlanta's leading feminists, was
quoted in the papers.

"We are getting very good feedback. People are not
saying, 'Oh, my God, all those women . . . here?' Five
years ago, they would have said that."

I happened to be hanging out at the Longhorn Steak-
house on Peachtree Street with a few of the guys during the
feminists' convention.

I asked my friend Rigsby, local observer of the political
and social scene and former mechanic at Marvin's One
Stop Transmission Shop before he decided to get into ob-
serving, what he observed about the meeting of the National Women's Political Caucus then in progress.

"Oh, my God," he observed. "All those women here?"

Sadly, there are those men who remain chained to out-
dated feelings about women, and I took it upon myself to
play the part of liaison between Atlanta's less progressive
males and our visiting sisters.

Here is what I told Rigsby and the guys at the Longhorn:

—If you happen to run into one of the visiting feminists

at a local drinkery this weekend, do not use your normal greetings to the opposite sex.

"You mean like, 'Hiya, baby!'?" asked Rigsby.

"Exactly," I said, "and especially don't use 'Hey, Chickee, Chickee,' because some of the more militant feminists often carry tire tools in their knapsacks."

—Never use the term "kitchen" around feminists.

"They don't think their place is in the house?" asked Rigsby.

"No," I replied. "It's the Senate and the Oval Office they're after now."

—Never attempt to buy any of these women a drink, because they are all self-supporting and have a great deal of pride.

"What about offering them some of my Red Man chew?" asked Rigsby.

"No way," I said. "Wait for them to ask for it first."

—If any of these women ask your stand on ERA, reply, "Fernando Valenzuela always has a good one," which will confuse them momentarily and give you time to make your escape before they decide you're trying to be cute and become enraged at your overt insensitivity to their needs and desires.

"Think you guys can handle all that?" I asked.

"You can count on us," said Rigsby. "Please tell the visiting feminists we hope they have a pleasant stay in our city and if there is anything we can do to help them reach their goal of equality, please don't hesitate to ask."

"What wonderful strides you guys are making," I said.

"Yeah," said Rigsby, "I don't want to get hit by no tire tool."

She Gets the Seesaw Treatment

T HE RECENT SNOW IN MY HOMETOWN CAUSED SEVERAL trees to fall in Susan Whiteside's yard.

Susan, who is twenty-six, and a former gymnast, decided she would deal with the fallen trees on her own rather than spend the money to have the work done for her.

She went out to rent a chain saw.

"It took me a while to locate a place," Susan was explaining, "but I finally found a store that rents chain saws. I just wanted the saw for a day."

"I'd like to rent a chain saw," Susan said to the man at the store.

The man said, "I'm sorry, but we can't rent chain saws to women. You could get hurt with a tool like that."

"I couldn't believe my ears," Susan went on. "This is 1987."

Susan pleaded her case—"I'm in top physical condition"—but she never did get her chain saw.

There have been thousands—yeah, even millions—of stories of sexual discrimination but I can't recall one of this nature.

Woman wants a chain saw. Woman can't rent chain saw because she's a woman.

I contacted the store and asked the man who answered the phone if he remembered a young woman who had tried to rent a chain saw from him.

He said he did.

"And why didn't you rent her one?" I asked.

The man, who identified himself as "one of the mechanics," was quite direct and seemingly honest with his answers.

"A chain saw can be a dangerous tool," he said. "And anybody can get hurt by one, especially a woman."

"Why 'especially a woman'?" I asked.

"They are not strong enough to start one, and even if they could, the engine can kick in so hard it could break their arm.

"We used to try to let women see if they could start a saw, but none of them ever could, and it seemed to embarrass them when they couldn't, so we stopped doing that too."

I asked if there were any special circumstances under which a woman might be able to rent a chain saw.

"If one comes in here with her husband or boyfriend who's willing to take responsibility, then no problem," said the mechanic.

"Or, if some four-hundred-pound woman wrestler came in here, I'd rent her a saw."

I wanted some reaction to this unusual situation from the regional office of the National Organization for Women, but when I phoned I got a recording. They probably were all out splitting logs.

I'm torn here. As a longtime champion of women's rights, I say if the lady wants a chain saw rent her a chain saw.

On the other hand, recall what happened when somebody rented Lizzie Borden an ax.

Judy and the Spider

JUDY IS TWENTY-SEVEN, AND SHE JUST GOT A DIVORCE after nine years of marriage. For the first time in her life, she is faced with learning how to become an independent woman.

Life used to be so simple. Grow up, get married, have children, join the Junior League.

But now there is rampant divorce and there are women seeking careers over families and there is Judy, who dropped into a world with which she is totally unfamiliar.

"I got married young," she was telling me. "I was eighteen. My parents took care of me up until then, and then I had my husband. This is the first time in my life I've really been on my own. It's a little scary."

I doubt there are very many people who aren't afraid of something. I'm afraid of snakes, dentists and airplanes when they are flying through bad weather.

Judy is afraid of spiders.

"I don't know why," she said. "But ever since I was a little girl, I just couldn't handle spiders."

Up until her recent divorce her problems with spiders had not been that difficult to handle.

"First, I had my daddy to take care of the spiders, and then I had my husband," Judy said. "I've even had him come home from work to kill a spider for me. Or, if I saw one in a room, I would lock the door and seal the spider inside. Then, when my husband came home, he would kill it for me."

Then, the divorce. One day, Judy is there, in the house, and there is no husband or daddy to call.

"I know this sounds silly," she said, "but a couple of days after we separated, it occurred to me I no longer had a man to call if there was a spider in the house. I tried to rationalize. I kept thinking maybe there won't be spiders in the house anymore. But I wasn't that lucky.

"I was walking through the living room and I looked down at the floor and crawling across the carpet was a big spider.

"I nearly freaked out. It was the biggest, ugliest spider I had ever seen. At first I nearly panicked. But then it occurred to me that if I didn't learn how to handle this thing with spiders, I never would become a totally independent woman.

"I put on a pair of high heels, and I went to the kitchen and got a broom. If I couldn't kill the spider from long range, with the broom, I figured I could stab it with one of the heels of my shoes.

"Just as I was ready to swat the spider with the broom, it crawled under the door of the laundry room. I thought to myself, 'I don't want to go in there with that spider,' but I knew I would never be able to go to sleep knowing there was a spider in the house.

"I opened the door to the laundry room, slowly, and the spider was right there in the middle of the room, and I swear it was staring at me, daring me to come any closer.

"I beat the spider with the broom for fifteen minutes. Then, I stepped on it with both high heels. I wanted to make certain it was dead.

"When the ordeal was over, and I had successfully defended myself against the spider, without a man helping me, I knew I could handle being alone. I knew I was finally an independent woman."

Admit it. You never get great stuff like this on *Donahue*.

Men Buying a Lady a Drink

SHE SAT ACROSS THE MOTEL BAR, CUTE AS SHE COULD be, sipping on her drink and reading from a paperback, possibly a romance novel featuring steaming passion and that sort of thing.

The place was crowded with weary travelers, and the band was too loud.

Two men in suits tried her first, but she would not even look up from her paperback. They went back to their table and sat down.

The man sitting next to me, who looked to be in his late twenties, had been watching her during a couple of martinis, both of which he had insisted come with two olives.

He made his first move.

"See the blonde behind you, the one reading the book?" he said to the bartender. "What's she drinking?"

"Whiskey sour," said the bartender.

"Send her one on me," said the man.

The girl didn't acknowledge receipt of the drink when it arrived in front of her. She simply pushed her old glass away, took a sip from the new one and went back to the paperback.

The man ordered another two-olive martini and waited.

The band rocked on. My ears ached.

Maybe twenty minutes passed, and the man sitting next to me hailed the bartender again.

"Send the lady another whiskey sour," he said.

I wondered why more bartenders didn't write books. They see and hear so much.

Again the girl didn't look up to see who her benefactor might be.

If it had been me I would have quit right there, but I was never any good in bars in the first place.

I heard "Buzz off, creep" a few times, which killed my confidence, and without his confidence, a man is no match for a woman in a dimly lit arena.

The band announced a slow song.

The guy sitting next to me was off his bar stool in a heartbeat. He went directly to the girl reading the book and asked her to dance.

They danced closely, and when the music ended they returned to the bar and he sat down beside her and ordered still another whiskey sour and they seemed to be getting along famously. After a few moments, she excused herself and walked out of the room. The man sat there as if he was expecting her to return. I figured her for a quick trip to the ladies room.

The man waited and he waited, but she never came

back. Finally, he summoned his tab. As he walked past me, he muttered something about the entire female gender.

I watched as the whiskey sour lover disappeared out of the door and headed back to his room—probably to call his wife.

THE MECHANICAL AGE: COMPUTERS, ANSWERING MACHINES AND HAIR DRYERS

***

A Special Place in Heaven

THERE SHOULD BE A SPECIAL PLACE IN HEAVEN FOR PEOPLE who do not have telephone answering devices, one of the most annoying mechanisms to be brought forth out of modern technology.

Americans will buy most anything you can plug into a wall that will perform what the average person could do quite easily.

Remember we are the country that gave the world the electric toothbrush, the hot comb, and Magic Fingers mattresses that still can be found at any motel where they advertise "Free TV" and offer an hourly rate.

A man said to me recently, "I wonder what we did before there was television remote control."

I'll tell you what we did. We got off our lazy duffs and we walked over to the television and changed the channels ourselves. That's all the exercise some people got.

Now, we just aim the remote control, and, like magic, the channel changes, making it possible to watch three football games, two soap operas and a Jerry Falwell sermon basically at the same time while our bodies deteriorate and become bloblike.

Besides the obvious interest in gadgets, I think most people install telephone answering machines for two reasons: Either they want others to think they get a lot of important calls and can't leave the phone unattended, or they don't want to miss out on the opportunity to be creative when it comes to making up a recorded message with which the machine answers.

Most try to put in a little would-be humor.

"Hi. This is Fernando. I can't come to the phone right now because I am on special assignment for the CIA, blah, blah, blah."

I call long distance and I still have to pay for the call because Fernando's stupid machine answered the phone. Nothing funny about that.

I've even heard answering machines do impressions:

"You dotty rat, you killed my bruddah, but I'll still call you back if you'll leave your name and numbah."

Why should I get a James Cagney impression when I call my chiropractor?

I must admit that because I was the victim of some bad advice, I recently purchased a telephone answering device. It was supposed to make my life easier. It didn't.

In the few days I kept it, however, I did learn a few things:

—Most people are too smart to talk to a machine, so they hang up as soon as they realize they are talking to one.

—The only people who will leave a message are those who want you to do something you don't want to do anyway.

—If your mother calls and a machine answers the phone, she either is afraid something is wrong with you or that you are doing something you shouldn't be doing.

I returned my answering machine and got my money back. I immediately phoned the Reverend Falwell to see if I still had a shot at the special place in heaven.

"Hi. This is the Reverend Jerry Falwell," began his recorded answer. "I can't come to the phone right now because I'm on special assignment for the CIA . . ."

I hung up. Heaven can wait.

Computers Writing Letters

THERE OUGHT TO BE A LAW AGAINST COMPUTERS WRITing letters to people.

I get letters from computers that belong to politicians,

television preachers and others who are begging for my money.

Computers attempt to make you think you have received these letters from a real person. They start out very chatty and they tell you how special you are to be receiving such a letter.

They can't fool me. I know when a computer has written me a letter every time because it usually fouls up my name.

"Dear Mr. Grozzard," a computer wrote to me recently.

I also know I'm not special because I am receiving a letter from a computer. I just happen to have made a few mailing lists here and there, probably because I ordered a set of Ginsu knives and a pocket fisherman off television.

Lee Southwell, a thirty-four-year-old lawyer who lives in Atlanta, Georgia, feels as I do about receiving letters from computers, especially after the two that came to him recently from two automobile dealerships there.

The first letter said he was a very special customer and if he would come down for a test drive he would receive a gift.

The second letter said if he just showed up on the lot with the letter he would receive a free oil painting and if he just happened to buy a car while he was there, he would receive four free oil paintings.

Lee Southwell didn't go to either place to test drive a car or to buy one in order to get the prizes, however, and for a good reason.

He is legally blind.

"I was tempted to go," he said. "I was going both places with my dog in his harness. I wanted to embarrass them."

Southwell has retinitis pigmentosa and has been legally blind for ten years. He has never been able to drive. He walks with the help of a black Labrador.

He was able to read the two letters from the auto dealerships by using an electronic aid that magnifies objects a thousand times and projects them onto a large television screen.

"I guess if I had a chip on my shoulder," he said, "I would really be insulted by these letters. But they have reminded me of my problem with mobility. The entire process is stupid and I don't guess there is anything we can do about them, because you can't outlaw stupidity."

No, but you can't sit still and do nothing, either, so I called the two car dealers and told them about Lee Southwell.

Both said the letters were mailed for them by outside concerns, but they also said they would do their best to take Lee Southwell's name off their list of potential customers.

It's a minor victory in the continuing struggle between man and computer, but I'll take it.

Computer Calling Scams

I WAS IN THE BED ASLEEP. THE PHONE RANG.

I picked it up and said a groggy "Hello." When I am awakened by the telephone I sound a little like Francis the talking mule, or so I've been told.

A voice came through from the other end, a taped voice. Once again, I was being victimized by one of those computer calling schemes. You answer the phone and some taped message is trying to sell you something.

I don't want anybody knocking on my door trying to sell me anything because if I was in the mood to buy something, I would go to a store.

Soliciting at my home is a violation of my privacy.

And so is calling me on the phone to try to sell me something. When such a thing occurs, I become quite angry and begin to curse at the voice on the other end of the phone until I realize the voice is a tape and can't hear itself being raked across a bed of verbal coals.

The tape the other morning gave me a number to call if I wanted to take advantage of some alleged bargain.

I took down the number and called it.

A woman answered and said, "Are you phoning about our special offer?"

"No," I said, "I'm phoning about the fact a computer just called me and a taped voice woke me up, and I want to talk to a live person in order to vent my anger for this outrage with words too timid for a carpenter who just hit his thumb with a hammer."

I was put on hold for several moments.

Then a man came on the line and identified himself as Ed Marks of a firm called United Systems.

I told Mr. Marks I didn't appreciate his company calling me.

As it turned out, Mr. Marks was a nice man. He apologized for the inconvenience and explained how his computer got my number, which is unlisted.

"The computer is programmed to dial numbers at random," he began, "so even if you have an unlisted number you can still get calls.

"We are a marketing firm that businesses contract for this sales technique. The call you received was an effort to get you to attend a presentation concerning a time-sharing vacation plan."

I told Mr. Marks I thought the technique was a lousy one and I asked him what I could do to avoid getting these calls that are becoming more and more common.

"Tell me your number," he said, "and I guarantee you won't be called by this company again."

Mr. Marks suggested that any time anybody receives such a call and wants such ceased, they do what I did. Call the number and raise the roof and tell them to tell their computer to go bother somebody else.

"If a company persists in calling you," Mr. Marks said, "you have a case against them for harassment."

So do it, folks. Call the jerks back when the computer calls you and tell them to leave you the hell alone.

If that doesn't work, find out who's in charge, get his or her phone number, and then call them at two in the morning and ask them if they would like to buy a mule.

Phones on Planes

ON CERTAIN COMMERCIAL FLIGHTS, AIRLINE PASSENGERS now may make phone calls back to the planet Earth. I was on one of those flights recently.

There was a portable phone on the wall near the galley. The flight attendant said if anybody wanted to use the phone, they simply could insert their credit card in the proper spot and then take the phone back to their seat.

I considered making a call. There wasn't anybody I particularly needed to talk to, but I thought it would be fun to try to impress the person sitting next to me.

I would dial the "800" number for Amtrak reservations, which nobody ever answers. I would pause for a few moments and then say, "Hello, Mr. President? Grizzard here returning your call. A meeting with Secretary Shultz at ten in the morning? I would be delighted to be there, sir, and give my best to Mrs. Reagan."

I decided such a ploy was fruitless, however, since the passenger next to me was some kid wearing one of those Walkman things in his ear. Every time he opened his mouth to yawn, I could hear some strange sort of music coming out, likely being played by a punk rocker with orange hair.

I suppose telephones in airplanes were bound to come sooner or later. In fancy hotels, they even have telephones in the guests' rest rooms nowadays, which isn't such a bad idea when you consider that studies indicate nine out of ten times you walk into your rest room either to take a shower or to relieve yourself, the telephone will ring.

I don't, however, like the idea of phones in planes. The only thing I liked about flying in the first place was it enabled me to get away from telephones for a few hours.

You see, I suffer from a condition known as Black Cord Fever, a disease that is at its worst around midnight, especially if the victim has had several drinks.

What happens is the victim has this overwhelming urge to talk to somebody on the telephone, even if it means waking them from a deep sleep. The problem is that very few people want to talk to a Black Cord Fever victim in the middle of the night.

The long-range effects of this condition are that the victim encounters huge telephone bills and finds his or her list of friends dwindling away.

I can see myself on a late night flight now. I've had a few beers, and I get hit by an attack of Black Cord Fever. I grab the phone on the plane and start dialing. A weary voice finally answers.

"Guess where I'm calling from?" I begin.

"A bar."

"No, Zero, I'm calling from an airplane! What do you think about that?"

"Get out of my life."

"Want to hear the engines?"

Click.

What the airlines are going to have to do if they insist on having phones on their planes is to remember those of us with Black Cord Fever.

"Phoning or nonphoning?" the ticket agent should ask.

"Nonphoning," I will reply and retire to the back of the airplane with the others so afflicted.

Electric Hair Dryers

I TOOK A LONG LOOK AT MY ELECTRIC HAIR DRYER THE other morning. It was a gift, and I cherished it once. Its sleek, modern styling hinted macho but at the same time said its owner would be a man of sensitivity, a man in touch with the necessity for good grooming habits.

I recall how the handle felt in my hand the morning of that first day. It fit perfectly. It was a part of me, an added appendage for countless mornings to come.

I began in warm, shifted to medium in mid-dry and then gunned it to high for the finish. My hair fluffed as it had never fluffed before. One spark, however, and meet the human torch.

I realize there are a number of important issues that probably should be discussed in a forum such as this, but occasionally the real issues of the day are hidden deep behind the headlines, and, occasionally, one must stand and be heard on a matter that at first glance might seem trivial.

The time has come, America, to speak out on the electric hair dryer for men.

It came to me as I stood, nerd-like, holding my dryer to my head. Like all mornings, I had showered and shampooed with a shampoo the fragrance of blossoming apricots, the color of the dawning sky.

This, I thought, is ridiculous. This is insane. This is a horrid, useless waste of time I can do without.

I figure I have spent five minutes every morning for the past five years blow-drying my hair. That is six days of my life spent with Flash Gordon's ray gun pointed at my brain, which probably has windburn by now.

It all began with cosmetics commercials screaming at us on television. Our forefathers rallied behind "54-40 or Fight!" and "Remember the Alamo!" and "A Chicken in Every Pot!" For this generation, it has been, "The Wethead Is Dead!" Pour out your Wildroot Creme Oil, Charlie, it's a blow-dry kind of day.

What followed was a mad rush by America's male population to grow hair. Then dry it. Then spray it so it wouldn't budge in a hurricane. No longer did men comb their hair. They raked it. Hair wasn't "cut," it was "styled."

Ears disappeared from Maine to California, and ten million bottles of Vitalis sat lonely and gathering dust, an oily relic of the past.

Young and old alike, we all bought electric hair dryers. Even athletes and probably truck drivers.

I know not what course others may take, but as for me, I have plugged in my electric hair dryer for the last time.

I despise the effort and time wasted on it, and I despise its high-pitched hum. Put an electric hair dryer to your head and you couldn't hear the 7:05 flight to Cleveland take off in the kitchen.

Left completely alone, I have discovered, hair will dry itself in less than an hour. I will save time, conserve energy and never be mistaken for a skinny sheepdog again.

I threw my electric hair dryer in the garbage, along with my banana cream rinse somebody said would give my hair body. I don't want body. I also tossed my shampoo that smells like blossoming apricots. The fragrance of blossoming apricots is for girls and boys who drink whiskey sours and eat the cherries.

Join me if you dare, men. Wetheads, arise again and stand tall! If you must, even slick it down and part it on the side and look up your old barber.

You never know. He may still be in business.

Computer Phobia

A UNIVERSITY OF CONNECTICUT STUDY HAS INDICATED that at least 25 percent of the population suffers from something known as computer anxiety.

Put simply, the results of the study mean that 25 percent of us feel like throwing up every time we hear about or are confronted with computers.

Why is this? The study answered that as well.

It said computer phobia is caused by a number of things, such as the fear computers might take one's job, the fear that a person might not be able to learn to operate the computer successfully and even the fear of somehow breaking one of the expensive mechanisms.

I suppose my friends and colleagues would find out sooner or later anyway, so I might as well go ahead and admit I am afflicted with computer anxiety myself.

I do all my work on a 1959 model manual typewriter. It won't do anything but type words on a sheet of paper, but quite frankly that's all I need it to do.

"But with a word processor," people say to me, "you can store information, edit your copy right there on the screen, blah, blah, blah."

Yeah, and I could faint and break out in a painful rash, too.

I'm not certain when I first developed computer anxiety. Perhaps it goes back to my freshman year in college. At registration, they handed me a computer card for each class I selected.

On each card were the ominous words DO NOT BEND, FOLD, STAPLE, SPINDLE OR MUTILATE.

The cards didn't say what would happen to me if I bent, folded, stapled, spindled, or mutilated them, but the inference was that if I did somehow commit one or more of those transgressions against a card, a harsh and swift penalty would be forthcoming.

I maintained a constant vigil over my cards, but one of my fellow students got strawberry jam on one of his. We never were quite certain what happened to him, but rumor circulated he was taken to a vacant warehouse and flogged with blackboard erasers.

All those of us with computer anxiety ask is that you try to understand us.

Don't say things that might hurt our feelings such as referring to us as "backward" or "stupid" or "stubborn" or "air-brained boobs." We prefer to be called the "technically impaired."

Also, do not talk about computers when you are around us. We often turn violent when we tire of computer conversation, and we start looking around for something or somebody to bend, staple, spindle or mutilate.

If people who like and understand computers and those of us who despise them don't learn to coexist, then what very well might result is two separate societies, computer persons in one and the technically impaired in the other.

I would hate to see it come to that, but those of us in the minority on this issue must stand firm and alert our detractors that we have no desire to be around computers or to have computers infringe upon our lives any further than they already have.

And you can bet your floppy disk on it.

Vending Machines That Won't Work

I'VE BEEN CONSIDERING MEASURES TO TAKE AGAINST vending machines that refuse to work.

I haven't any concrete numbers, but I would guess that in the thirty or so years I've been feeding money into these callous contraptions, they actually have worked only about 50 percent of the time.

A few times when they don't work, the machine doesn't deliver the object I have selected, but it does return my money. I can deal with this.

What happens mostly, however, is the machine not only doesn't give me my soft drink or candy bar or bag of peanuts, it also refuses to return my money.

I cannot deal with this. My eyes bulge out, my hands begin to shake, and I want to kill the machine.

To this point, I have never taken any drastic measures, however, because of my fear of the men in the white coats with their butterfly nets.

Another source of my frustration when it comes to

vending machines is there never seems to be anybody around to scream at when a stupid machine has just ripped you off.

You would think, since the machine is in a hotel or a restaurant, you could go to some sort of assistant manager and say, in a loud voice so others could hear you, "Your blankety-blank machine has robbed me of my money!"

The problem is that when a vending machine refuses to work, it is impossible to find anybody who will take responsibility for it.

"We just lease the space to the vending company," I have been told.

"You'll have to talk to Mr. Wallakowski about that and he's on vacation in Wyoming and will not be back until 1989," is another copout.

It would be easier getting your money back from a television evangelist.

I decided, however, it is possible to get something back that is better than your money—revenge. Here is how I have planned to get back at the next vending machine that robs me.

1. I am going to kick the machine. I don't mean a gentle kick. I mean, I'm going to rare back and kick the machine until there are large dents in it. I am going to kick it until it is in a terrible state of disrepair and then I am going to spit on it and call it ugly names.

2. After that, I am going to get violent. I am going to my car and get my lug wrench and I am going to beat the machine some more. I want glass to fly. I want things inside the machine to make awful crunching sounds. I want nuts and bolts and screws to roll around on the floor. I want nearby dogs to whimper and small children to cry.

3. Then, I'm going to get really mad. I'm going to set the thing on fire. I am going to take off my clothes and dance naked around the smoldering machine, throwing my hands wildly into the air, while giving out primal screams.

And after a few days of quiet rest in my padded cell, I will emerge a new man.

NORTH VERSUS SOUTH

✳✳✳

A Funny Thing Happened in New York

A FUNNY THING HAPPENED TO ME IN NEW YORK DURING my recent visit. Everybody was nice to me.

I told a friend back home.

"That's impossible," he said. "You might occasionally find somebody who is nice to you when you visit New York, but not everybody."

Most people who don't live in New York think of it as the home office for obnoxious behavior.

"Never forget one time when I was in New York," a guy told me. "Went up to this fellow selling papers and asked if he could give me directions to the St. Regis Hotel.

"He looked at me and said, 'Outta here. I don't know nuttin' about nuttin'.'"

But perhaps New York is changing. Perhaps the Big Apple, or the people who live and work there, are reaching out to us now to say they are sorry for treating us so badly before.

I probably took six cab rides during my visit. Not a single driver refused to speak or grunted in disgust at the size of his tip.

I even had a driver indulge in a bit of pleasant conversation. He said, "Cold enough for you?"

I replied, "It's cold as a witch's . . ."

Well, my reply was quite cordial and when I told the driver to keep the change after I handed him three ones for a $2.20 fare, he actually said, "Thanks a lot, and have a nice day."

These are the mean streets of New York?

I went into a restaurant for lunch. I ordered a beer. I

expressly told the waiter not to pour my beer into a glass. I prefer my beer out of the bottle or can.

The waiter forgot and poured my beer into a glass anyway.

"I didn't want the beer in a glass," I said.

"I'm sorry, sir," said the waiter. "I forgot. Allow me to bring you another beer, and you will not have to pay for the first one. It was my fault."

You sure you're not in another city? I asked myself.

I was looking for a restaurant in which to have dinner. The cabbie couldn't find the restaurant.

I got out of the cab and asked a pedestrian if he knew where the restaurant was.

He politely told me where the restaurant was located and, recognizing I was a visitor, said, "Have a nice stay in the city."

This couldn't be happening.

I went into the restaurant. The coat check lady smiled when I checked my coat. The maitre d' was very pleasant in showing me to my table and didn't sneer at my clothes.

The waiter served dinner with a smile.

I finished my meal, reached into my pocket and pulled out the appropriate cash to pay the check.

As I stood outside the restaurant a short time later trying to hail another cab, the waiter came out and tapped me on the shoulder.

"Sir," he said. "I think you dropped this out of your pocket when you were paying your check."

It was a five-dollar bill. I was shocked. I told him to keep the five to go with his tip. He refused.

I thanked the waiter and got into my cab and went back to my hotel room. Somebody had turned my bed down and there was a piece of chocolate candy on the pillow.

For the first time ever, I slept with the lights off in New York.

All Shook Up by Culture Shock

THERE IS A GROUP OF ATLANTANS, FORMERLY NEW Yorkers, who have formed their own support group called "The New York Network." They get together to whine about all the things they miss about their hometown.

There was a story about the group in the Atlanta papers last week. It said these people missed such things as egg creams.

Quite frankly, I have no idea what an egg cream is, but as an Atlantan who was once held prisoner of war in Chicago, I know what it is like to be ravaged by homesickness.

I lived in Chicago for nearly three years. It was very cold there and the people talked funny.

One day, I met a guy in a bar who also was from the South. I knew that right away when I heard him ask a young lady seated next to him, "Do you think wrestlin's fake?"

Southerners are known for their ability to engage in clever repartee in such social situations as trying to pick up a date in a bar.

After the young lady moved several seats away from the man, I began talking with him. It turned out he was from Birmingham, Alabama, and he, too, was homesick.

He told me about a support group to which he belonged, "Grits Anonymous," for misplaced Southerners.

He invited me to attend the group's next meeting. It was wonderful. We filled up the host's Jacuzzi with grits and wallowed around in them until we all felt we could handle

Chicago and our homesickness until at least the next meeting.

After some research I found there are other groups of Atlantans who are transplanted Northerners and meet occasionally to deal with problems they have encountered since moving south. There is, for instance, the "Federation of Former New Jersey Americans," who miss such things as seeing bodies floating in rivers. They meet at Barney's Waterslide every other Wednesday.

"It's not what we're used to, of course," said the group's founder, Nick Valentino, from Newark, "but it does help some of our members to cope."

Then, there's "We're from Cleveland," people who never get to see rivers burn any more. What they do is rent a raft and float down Atlanta's scenic Chattahoochee River. At lunch time they pour gasoline on the water and roast wienies.

I even discovered a group of transplanted Chicagoans, "The Fruit Loops." Every time the temperature falls below 60 degrees they take off their clothes and run around outside in hopes of enjoying the invigorating feeling of frostbite once more.

What's obviously happening in our country is more and more people are leaving their roots to find their fortunes, and this obviously can lead to various forms of culture shock.

I eventually left Chicago for home because I could no longer handle a foreign way of life, and I am certain the people from New York and New Jersey and Cleveland and Chicago will be leaving the South and returning home soon, too.

Bye, y'all.

Southerners Learning Not to Speak Southern

THERE HAVE BEEN SEVERAL REPORTS RECENTLY OF southerners going to special classes in an effort to learn not to speak Southern.

I read of such classes in Atlanta, where people who took the course said they were afraid if they didn't stop talking with a Southern accent, it might impede their progress toward success.

A young woman who works for IBM said, "I want to advance through the company (and) I feel I need to improve my voice...."

What she really was saying is the IBM office where she works is run by a bunch of northern transplants who probably make fun of the way she talks, and she is embarrassed and wants to talk like they do.

That, in my opinion, is grounds for loss of Southern citizenship.

What are we trying to do here? Do we all want to sound like those talking heads on local television news who have tried so hard not to have an accent, their vocal chords are nervous wrecks?

What's wrong with having a Southern accent? My grandfather said "y'all" (only in the plural sense, however, as Yankees have never figured out) and my grandmother said, "I reckon." And if IBM doesn't like that kind of talk, they can just program themselves right back to where they came from.

I like accents. I like to try to emulate accents, other than my own.

I do a big-time Texas oilman: "Now, you ladyfolks just

run along 'cause us menfolk got to talk about bidness."

I can even talk—or at least type—like Bostonians sound: "Where can I pock my cah?"

The wonderful thing about the way Americans treat the English language is we have sort of made it up as we have gone along, and I see absolutely nothing wrong with having different ways to pronounce different words.

New Yorkers say "mudder and fadder."

Midwesterners say, "mahmee and dee-ad."

Southerners say, "mahma and deadie."

Big deal.

If we all spoke the same, dressed the same, acted the same, thought the same, then this country would not be the unique place that it is, would not have the benefit of our spice and variety, and everybody probably would be in the Rotary Club.

What we all need to realize is the more diverse we are, the stronger we are. Being able to get second and third and even fourth and fifth opinions often will prevent the nastiest of screw-ups.

I say if you are going to classes to lose your Southern accent, you are turning your back on your heritage, and I hope you wind up working behind the counter of a convenience store with three Iranians and a former Indian holy man.

And if you happen to be from another part of the country and make fun of the way Southerners talk, may you be elected permanent program chairman of your Rotary Club.

Y'all reckon I've made my point?

Marching Again On Atlanta

THE DEMOCRATS HAVE MADE A PERFECT CHOICE IN picking Atlanta for their 1988 national convention.

Atlanta often has hosted the Shriners and once every two years, Clemson fans come to town to watch their football team play Georgia Tech.

And here's another thought: The Democrats long have been noted for their disorganization, and Atlanta isn't screwed on that tightly at the moment, either. We've got a mayor who spends more time in Africa than he does at City Hall, we've got taxi cabs that couldn't qualify for the demolition derby, and the city is growing so fast it looks like Sherman came back and this time he had bulldozers and jackhammers.

And personally, I'd much rather cover a Democratic convention in Atlanta than a Republican convention.

Republicans compared to Democrats are dull. At the Republican convention in Detroit in 1980, I noted all the Republicans seemed very happy and looked a lot alike.

The way I could pick out a Republican delegate was to see if he were wearing a sweater with the name of a country club embroidered on the front, or if she carried a Gucci bag and had a tan.

The only real excitement at the Republican convention in 1980 happened when a group of women who didn't have Gucci bags or tans marched in protest because the Republicans hadn't included a pro-ERA plank in their platform.

I didn't cover the march because I was afraid to, but one of my newsroom colleagues did.

When he returned, he had a hole in his jacket.

"What happened to your jacket?" somebody asked him.

"I was interviewing one of the marchers and she dropped her cigar on my jacket and burned a hole in it," he explained.

Later in the summer, in New York, the Democrats got together and made the Republican gathering look like a Tupperware party.

Among the groups shouting and protesting and looking very unhappy were the no-nukes, gays-for-Kennedy, and defenders of baby whales. There was also a guy with orange hair who was roller skating in front of the Statler Hilton Hotel—on behalf of roller skates.

I got a little crazy, too, and decided to interview a delegate from Guam who was wearing a straw hat. He didn't say anything that made very much sense, but he did thank me for being the first newsperson ever to interview anybody from the Guam delegation.

I heard Jimmy Carter say "Hubert Horatio Hornblower" when he meant to say Hubert Horatio Humphrey and I saw Rosalynn Carter give Teddy Kennedy, who had challenged her husband for the nomination, a glare that would have put Kennedy in traction for six months if looks could maim; and I paid $14 for a cheeseburger.

Atlanta will have something like that for the Democrats in '88, too. Local restaurants will offer the same special for conventioneers they put on for Clemson fans: all the fried chicken you can eat for $69.95.

Y'all come.

Life Span in Georgia

A RECENT STUDY OF THE LIFE SPANS OF MEN AND women showed that Georgia is near the bottom in a ranking of states.

Hawaii and Minnesota were the states where people live the longest.

Hawaii, of course, features a warm tropical climate where people sit around drinking various exotic concoctions made with pineapple juice and watch lovely young girls in grass skirts move their sensuous bodies to ukulele music.

The only drawback to living a long time in Hawaii is you get very old and your eyesight eventually goes, so you can no longer see the young girls move their bodies, but you still have to put up with all that ukulele music.

As to Minnesota, nobody really lives a long time there. It's so cold it just seems like it.

Being a Georgian, I naturally was concerned upon discovering I can't expect to live as long as people from other states.

Georgia is a marvelously diverse state, with mountains and seashores and charming small towns and, of course, bustling exciting Atlanta.

So what makes us die earlier than other Americans? I put some thought to this question and came up with the following:

ATLANTA TRAFFIC—Other cities have traffic jams; Atlanta has traffic wars. General Sherman burned this city. The highway department is dismantling it, piece by piece.

There is so much highway construction in Atlanta, motorists have to wear hard hats. Rather than face another day in Atlanta traffic, a lot of people simply die to avoid it.

GNATS—Gnats, tiny bugs, are the cause of a number of deaths in south Georgia each year. Some of these deaths have been attributed to swallowing a large number of gnats while talking or eating.

Some also think the reason a lot of south Georgians disappear and never are heard from again is they are carried off by giant swarms of gnats and drowned in the Oke-fenokee Swamp.

KUDZU—Nothing grows faster than a kudzu vine. It has been known to cover entire homes in Georgia while the families are asleep for the night. They are then trapped inside and can't get to a convenience store, so they starve.

Those who try to eat their way out of kudzu quickly have their innards entangled in the vine, because no matter how much you chew it, the blamed stuff just keeps on growing.

THE FALCONS—The Falcons lost a game to the Chicago Bears, 36–0, and the Falcons' coach blamed it on poor officiating. The Falcons have been big losers most every year they've been in Atlanta. A man fell out of the stadium during a Falcons game once and was killed. I think he jumped after another Falcons holding penalty.

LIVING IN BUCKHEAD—Buckhead is a tiny section of Atlanta, similar to those in other large metropolitan areas, where about eleven million white people under the age of thirty-five live.

Each evening, all eleven million get into their Mercedeses and go to trendy Buckhead bars and talk to one another. Here is what a Buckhead bar conversation usually sounds like:

"I was like, 'Wow!' and he was like, 'Really?'"

These people might die from wearing their designer jeans too tight, choking on hearts of palm while eating their salads or being trampled by a polo pony.

The study further revealed at what time of year most Georgians die. It's when the state legislature is in session.

Unsophisticated in Reagansville

WASHINGTON—PUBLIC TELEVISION WAS DOING A series of programs entitled "Back of the Book" in which various individuals were to sit around a table and discuss matters pertaining to books, movies, television, music and the media.

The group invited to Washington to participate included:

—The rock music critic of *Rolling Stone*.

—The television critic of the *Chicago Tribune*, a woman.

—An editor from *Adweek*, also a woman, who agreed with most everything the lady TV critic from Chicago said.

—An erudite professor from Amherst, where the debate team probably gets more attention than the football squad.

—The movie critic of the *Washington Post*, who wears glasses with red rims.

—A man from Chicago who identified himself as a "political satirist." Great work, I suppose, if you can get it.

—And me. I wasn't certain why I had been asked to take part in the discussions, but when I told the TV critic from Chicago I lived in Atlanta, was a graduate of the University of Georgia and thought George Jones was the best thing to come along since sliced bread, she said, "Oh, then you must be our local yokel."

That was my first clue I probably wasn't going to fit in here. For the next three days, I went head to head with this group of sophisticates, none of whom ever agreed with a single thing I said. I haven't felt that out of place since I walked into Brooks Brothers looking for a pair of jeans.

We were talking about subway vigilante Bernhard Goetz, for instance. Everybody else said they thought he was sick and should be put under the jail.

I said I thought he was a great American hero for striking back against crime and that Roy Rogers would have done the same thing if four thugs had messed with him on a subway. You should have heard their howls of disgust.

We talked about *The New Yorker* magazine. The professor from Amherst said anybody who didn't read it probably attended the University of Georgia.

I said I didn't think it was so hot because I went to a cocktail party given by *The New Yorker* once and they didn't have any beer. All they served was white wine, which I pointed out is the favorite drink of wimps and feminists with chips on their shoulders.

We talked about our favorite movies. Somebody said theirs was Rainer Werner Fassbinder's immortal *Marriage of Maria Braun*.

I said mine was *Walking Tall*, where Joe Don Baker takes apart a bar with a big stick. I thought the movie critic from the *Post* was going to faint.

We also discussed the explicit lyrics of rock star Prince. The man from *Rolling Stone* said that's just the way young people are these days. I said the only good thing about Prince is now we don't have to spend a lot of tax money on sex education in our schools. Just give every kid a Prince album.

Finally, the moderator asked each member of the panel for any closing thoughts.

My fellow panel members discussed all sorts of issues I didn't understand and the professor from Amherst said that anybody who would drink beer at a *New Yorker* cocktail party wasn't socially fit to attend a hog-slopping.

When it came my turn, I said, "How about them Dawgs!" and caught the first bus home.

FAMILY/
CHILDHOOD

�֎�֎�֎

The Last Time I Saw Dawson

I WAS DRIVING HOME FROM SOUTH GEORGIA ON A TWO-lane road. The scenery was acres of freshly plowed fields, rows of tall corn and an occasional old dog asleep on a front porch.

Towns I passed through hadn't changed since the last time I passed through them. That's one of the things I like about small towns.

They have names like Sasser and Dawson and Parrot and Richland. Sasser I know little about. They filmed a western movie in Parrot once. I'll bet nobody gets in much of a hurry in Richland.

The last time I was in Dawson, we buried a good friend.

The thought came to me as I drove along that I've been an urban animal, away from slow paces and open spaces, for a long time now. In fact, I've been out of the slow lane longer than I lived in it.

It's changed me. It changes all of us who leave home, for bigger, and, presumably, better things.

I don't sleep as well as I used to when I was back in my mother's house, curled up under those quilts my grandmother made with failing eyes and arthritic hands.

New sights don't open my eyes as widely as they once did. And I catch myself nowadays in about as many cynical moods as sentimental ones, and I hurry more often than I cruise.

Fools rush in and fools rush on, I suppose, and they often are afraid to give up the night.

As I drove on, noting the onrushing growth of the kudzu, the plush pecan groves and peach orchards and the absence of billboards, I wondered what it would be like to

53

go back and live in a place where they don't lock their doors at night and there are more hours in a day than you really need.

Would I be bored in that sort of environment? Sometimes yes, but boredom does have its good points. It allows the opportunity to reflect and savor and play with the mind. When I was a boy, I spent a lot of time just with me and my imagination.

I made up baseball games and I silently broadcast them to myself. I fought wars, ran races, caught large fish and held girls in bright sundresses.

I wondered what it would be like to live in a town again where I knew everybody and liked most of them and was able to place every dog with its owner.

I don't even know my own neighbors now, and I can't even name my own dog's friends.

Some people never search for dreams that await outside their city limits. I used to think people like that were cowards.

I've changed my mind on that now, however. There was a song with the line: "I don't know which takes more courage, the staying or the running away."

And somebody once said to me, "You spend the first half of life trying to get away from home and the second half trying to get back." There is some truth to that, I said to the highway in front of me. There really is.

September 1957 Photo

I WAS GOING THROUGH SOME OLD BOXES I'VE HAD IN storage, and I ran across a black-and-white photograph of my stepfather, my mother and me.

The date on the photograph was September 1957. I was eleven. I had a flattop haircut and my ears stuck out.

I had forgotten my ears stuck out when I was a kid. My

friends called me Dumbo, after the flying elephant who used his mammoth ears for wings.

Thank the Lord long hair over the ears later became fashionable for men, and I think my face also grew wider, so my ears don't stick out nearly as much as they once did.

It's been nearly twenty-eight years since we had that picture taken. My mother used to say things like, "You'll be surprised how fast the years pass by once you get older."

I didn't believe her at the time.

My mother. She looks so young and strong in that picture. Her hands are resting on my shoulders. I remember those hands so vividly. They were warm, loving hands that could turn into lethal weapons when applied forcefully to my backside.

In that picture my mother looks like I will always remember her. Today she is very sick and very weak. Damn age, how it ravages.

I am older now than my stepfather was when we had that picture taken. That's hard to believe.

He was stern with me, but he was also kind. The one gesture I will never forget was that when I graduated from high school, he allowed my real father to take his seat and sit next to my mother to watch me receive my diploma.

There is not a great deal of landscape pictured around us, but I know exactly where we were when the photograph was snapped.

You don't forget trees you climbed as a boy, or gravel driveways where you hit rocks into the cornfield with a broomstick. I played a million fantasy baseball games in that driveway, which separated my grandmother's house from my aunt's.

I sat down and looked at the photograph for a long time, and what I realized was that I was wrong about adulthood back when I was a child.

I thought that when I became an adult, all my problems would cease. I wouldn't have anybody telling me what I could or couldn't do. I wouldn't be afraid of snakes or the dark anymore. And I'm certain I even thought time would continue creeping at the pace it did when I was eleven and wanted desperately to be twelve.

I was dead wrong, as a matter of fact, and I had to ask myself an intriguing question: Would I trade all that I have now, including the experiences that aging brings, for the innocence on the eleven-year-old face in that photograph?

If I could just keep the ears I have now, most probably I would.

Guess What Happened in Moreland?

MORELAND, GEORGIA—"YOU'LL NEVER GUESS WHAT happened in Moreland," said my mother.

"They found marijuana growing down by the creek," she went on.

For a moment I thought my mother had said they had found marijuana growing down by the creek in Moreland, which, of course, couldn't happen in my little hometown of three hundred where life has remained calm and serene and where a major scandal is somebody mowing their lawn during Sunday church hours.

"I don't think I understand," I said to my mother.

"I said, 'They found marijuana growing in Moreland, down by the creek where you boys used to play,'" she responded in an unmistakably definitive tone.

I got all the details as to who was allegedly responsible for growing the illicit weed and how a helicopter had spotted the growth.

God, I thought to myself, what do we have here? An episode for *Moreland Vice*?

I suppose it was inevitable big-time crime eventually

would find Moreland. It finds most every other place.

But they still don't have a policeman in Moreland—nor a red light—and the only crime I remember in Moreland when I was a kid was three rowdy brothers breaking into Cureton and Cole's store and stealing some candy bars and soft drinks.

They were sentenced to six months of Sunday school at the Methodist church.

The first Sunday they beat up three primary kids, drank all the Kool-Aid and stole all the crayons, and when they didn't return the next Sunday, nobody dared contact the authorities for fear they would order the three rowdies back.

We did have a policeman once, a sort-of-policeman. Jake Starkins, a Baptist deacon, discovered there was a pool table in the back of Rainwater's service station, prayed on the matter and got the heaven-sent message to take whatever steps necessary to remove the pool table, thus saving Moreland and its children from what he was convinced would soon be galloping decadence if pool games were allowed to continue.

Jake declared himself constable of Moreland, painted a star on the side of his '53 blue Plymouth and stormed into Rainwater's, declaring he was on a mission from God and ordering the pool table removed from the premises.

Unfortunately for Jake and the morals of Moreland's children, the three aforementioned rowdy brothers were in the midst of a game of 9-ball when Jake appeared. They gave Jake a few on the top of his head with their cue sticks.

When he came to, Jake got back into his Plymouth and drove home. Neighbors said it took him less than fifteen minutes to remove the star from the side of his car.

That creek where they found the marijuana was a special place to me. We dammed it two or three times a week, we caught crawfish from it, and once I convinced Kathy Sue Loudermilk to meet me there.

Me and Kathy Sue alone at last in the wooded privacy

of the creek. Unfortunately, nothing noteworthy came of our rendezvous—a yellow jacket stung Kathy Sue and she ran home crying—but remembering the incident did make me feel a bit better about the recent drug scandal in Moreland.

Compared to what I was thinking about in regard to Kathy Sue that long ago day, growing a little marijuana becomes a forgivable misdemeanor indeed.

Mother's Birthday

MORELAND, GEORGIA—IT WAS MY MOTHER'S BIRTH-day, so a few members of the family gathered to help her celebrate. We gave up on my mother having too many more birthdays some time ago, but she's currently making another in a long series of comebacks.

My Aunt Jessie, who lives just past the clothesline from my mother, was there and brought some of her wonderful creamed corn. I ate myself under the table.

Anyway, since it was a birthday we were celebrating, the question of age came up. My Aunt Jessie said proudly she was seventy-five and she hoped and prayed to live to be a hundred, which she'll probably make. She stays too busy not to.

"Didn't you just have a birthday?" somebody asked me.

I admitted I did.

"How old were you?" asked my Aunt Jessie.

"Thirty-nine," I said.

I hadn't really thought a lot about birthdays until the subject was brought up at home. I hadn't thought much about reaching thirty-nine, either.

Thirty-nine. It certainly doesn't seem as old to me as it once did, but thirty-nine is sort of the year you have to admit you're losing the battle against time.

You fight time when you're younger. It passes much too slowly, but all of a sudden the years have sneaked away and there you stand on the threshold of forty, which is the year, if you're a single man, it's time you quit messing around with women who don't know how World War II came out.

"It doesn't seem like it's been thirty-nine years since you were born," said my Aunt Jessie, who is very outspoken. "I remember going to see you in the hospital. I believe you were the ugliest baby I've ever seen."

My mother was eating birthday cake and not paying attention, so there was nobody in the room to defend me.

"You were just a tiny thing and you had the reddest face," my aunt continued. "I thought at first there was something wrong with you."

"There was," said one of my cousins. I chose to ignore that remark.

My Aunt Jessie was just warming up concerning the secrets of my infancy.

"I baby-sat you all the time," she said, "and you were the worst one to get galded I've ever seen."

I didn't know what "galded" meant, so I asked my cousin.

"Getting a raw butt," she explained.

My aunt went on.

"I was trying to change you one day and I had a jar of Vaseline sitting on the table. I don't think you were a year old yet, but you picked up the jar of Vaseline and threw it across the room.

"It shattered into a thousand pieces and I popped you a good one right on your behind. I left my handprint on you, and I was scared to death your mama or daddy would see it, but they didn't. But I don't think you ever threw a jar of Vaseline again, either."

I haven't. As a matter of fact, every time I see a jar of Vaseline I get a severe pain in my . . . well, where my aunt popped me one.

Before the day was over, I decided not to be concerned
with the fact I'm turning thirty-nine and soon will be forty.
Anybody born as ugly as I was and who was subjected to
such cruelty as an infant is darn lucky to have made it this
far.

I'll Never Forget the Time...

WE ALL GO BACK A LONG WAY, AND QUITE NATURALLY
we begin telling war stories, the ones that inevitably begin
with "I'll never forget the time..."

We don't see each other that often anymore, and we
haven't seen each other's parents in years, and there is the
southern custom of asking about one's parents.

It goes, "How's your mamma and 'en (and them)?"—
which translates into, "In what condition are your mother
and your other first of kin?"

We took turns talking about our parents. "My mother
puts terrible guilt trips on me," somebody said. "I'll call
and tell her I'm on my way shopping, and she'll say, 'I
wish I had the money to go shopping.'"

"Mine does the same thing," said somebody else. "I
won a trip to Las Vegas from my company and I called my
mother and told her about it.

"She said, 'I guess that means you won't be coming to
see me in a long time.'

"I said, 'Mama, it's just for a week.' She said, 'I may
not be here another week.'

"She's in perfect health, but I called her every day from
Vegas just to make sure she hadn't contracted some sort of
terrible disease."

I said my mother still worries about whether or not I'm

wearing clean underwear because I might be in a wreck and the doctors would see my dirty undershorts.

"My mother does that, too," somebody else spoke up, "but it all means they really love us."

It does. It's funny how our attitudes change about our parents as we get older and they get older. These people were our enemies when we were children.

They were the ones who made us eat our vegetables, made us go to bed earlier than we wanted to, fussed over our grades, lectured us and wouldn't allow us out of the house with dirty underwear.

But you forget all that, and you would miss the guilt trips if your folks weren't around to send you on them.

"Tell them about your dad and the biscuits," one friend asked another.

"God, it still makes me cry," she began.

"Every morning when I go to work, I go right by my father's house. And every morning—I've been doing this for years—I stop by and drink coffee with him and he makes biscuits for me because he doesn't want me going to work on an empty stomach.

"One day I overslept, and I knew I wouldn't be able to stop by and see him. The weather was awful. It was cold and it was raining.

"So I called my dad and told him I wouldn't have time to stop by. He said, 'You won't?' I could hear the disappointment in his voice, but I said, 'Daddy, I'll stop by tomorrow morning, so don't worry about it.'

"So I get in the car and I start driving to work. As soon as I rounded the corner to drive past the house, I saw this figure standing out in the cold and rain with a sack in his hand.

"It was Daddy. He was out there waiting for me so I would still have my biscuits."

Everybody in the room was in tears when she finished. 'Tis the season to be thankful. Thanks for parental love, the purest love of all.

Lunch with Danny and Dudley

MORELAND, GEORGIA—I WAS HAVING LUNCH HERE IN my hometown with the folks, and Dudley Stamps and Danny Thompson, both of whom still live in these parts, dropped by.

We were boys together here, but we don't see very much of each other anymore. Twenty years ago we were inseparable. Then one day, I went my way and they went theirs.

Danny's hair is turning gray. Dudley is losing his. They both have good jobs and families. They seem happy.

So we had this idea after lunch, and that was to take a walk together. Grown men rarely take walks together, but the weather was nice and since we were in the midst of reminiscence anyway, it seemed the thing to do to take a walk around the little town from which we sprouted.

We walked slowly, and we stopped often. We told some old stories and we had us some laughs.

We were walking through what used to be my grandmother's yard where we played together before we learned our multiplication tables.

"Mama Willie's yard doesn't seem nearly as big as it did back then, does it?" said Danny.

It didn't. What, I wondered, is the shrinking agent in time?

We walked up to the Methodist church. The vacant lot in front of the church was where we played touch football.

The lot isn't vacant anymore. Somebody poured some concrete on it and put up a fence.

We walked down to Cureton and Cole's store, or to the building that used to be Cureton and Cole's store, where we met each afternoon after school and drank big orange bellywashers and ate Zagnut candy bars.

Cureton and Cole's store is now home to some sort of interior decorator. That hurt.

The post office isn't the post office anymore, either. It's a beauty salon, and they're trying to refurbish the old hosiery mill next store and make it into a museum.

We remembered the Fourth of July street dances they used to hold in front of the old hosiery mill.

"They quit having them," Danny said, "when folks got to drinkin' and fightin'."

"They're trying to bring them back, though," said Dudley. "Now, they smell your breath before they'll sell you a ticket."

We walked up what was left of the old path that leads to the schoolhouse. Danny peeked through one of the windows at the room where we spent our eighth grade year.

"Dang if that sight don't pull at my stomach," he said.

We had to go to the old ballfield. Dudley was our catcher. Danny played first. I pitched.

Even the ballfield wasn't the same. They've put home plate where right field used to be, and somebody tore down the tree that provided the shade for the home team bench.

The walk was over much too quickly. Back home, we talked about the inevitability of change and how they should have left our ballfield the way it was.

Then we shook hands and said we ought to do this sort of thing more often, which we won't, of course. But at least we had this day, the day three grown men walked back through their childhood together.

I wish I had told them how much I loved them before they left. But you know how grown men are.

Thanks for the Memory

It was three years ago, or maybe it was two. Thanksgivings come and Thanksgivings go.

I overslept and missed the family gathering at my uncle's house out in the country.

Country folks like to eat early, and like I said, I overslept.

B. A. called about one in the afternoon. He was down in Savannah, alone.

"Had lunch yet?" I asked him.

"I was just going to pick up a hamburger," he answered.

"No Thanksgiving feast?"

"No. I had some work to catch up on and couldn't get to Montgomery to my mother's. What are you doing?"

"No plans," I said.

"Catch a plane," B. A. said. "The Hyatt bar is open even if nothing else is."

I was at the Savannah airport three hours later.

We never made it to the Hyatt bar. We stopped instead at a little beer joint just outside the airport.

There were a couple of pool tables inside and young men wearing hats with the names of various heavy equipment companies sewn on them were playing. Cigarettes dangled from their mouths. They were silent and expressionless. One got the idea heavy stakes were involved.

A few old men sat around the bar drinking beer. A man and a woman worked behind the bar. There was a juke box playing country music.

"Keep your mouth shut," B. A. said, "and we'll probably be OK."

"Probably..."

We had a few beers and played a few tunes of our own. Nobody had spoken to us until a graybeard sitting a few stools down looked up from his can of beer and asked, "Y'all ain't from around here, are you?"

We said we weren't.

"Y'all going to stay for supper?" the man went on.

"Stay for what?" I asked.

"Supper," he said. "We have it here every year on Thanksgiving. It's mostly for the regulars who don't have nowhere else to go, but I'm sure nobody would mind if y'all stayed."

We didn't say yes. But we didn't say no, either.

A half hour later, the door to the joint opened and in walked five or six ladies bearing plates of food. Lots of food. They set up a table near the juke box. Turkey and dressing. A ham. Mashed potatoes and gravy. Green beans. Butterbeans. Creamed corn. Home-made rolls. There were also cakes and pies.

The customers put down their beers and pool sticks. They lined up plates in hand for the feast in front of them.

"Y'all more than welcome to eat," said the woman behind the bar. We got in line.

The food was wonderful. We went back twice.

"You do this every year, huh?" I asked one of the ladies that brought the food.

"They's lots of people don't have nowheres to go on Thanksgiving," she said. "Some of 'em come in here to drink cause it ain't as lonely as staying home. We all live in the neighborhood and we just try to share what we got with others."

We stayed until nine or ten. We tried to pay extra for the food, but nobody would take our money. Thanksgivings come and Thanksgivings go, and, occasionally, one comes along that is very special.

Lizards Need Love Too

IT'S BEEN MORE THAN TWENTY YEARS, BUT I'VE NEVER forgotten the pretty, blond girl who sat next to me in a class I had at the University of Georgia.

She wore lovely sweaters. The only days I didn't notice her lovely hair and her lovely eyes were the days she wore her lovely sweaters.

I wanted to speak to her, to ask her out. I wanted to take her to the Alps Road Drive-in Theater in my 1958 red and white Chevrolet.

"Lovely sweater you are wearing this evening, my dear," I would say, looking deeply into her lovely eyes, stroking her lovely hair.

She would grab me as her passion soared out of control and we would spend the entire double feature kissing squarely upon one another's mouth, which is as far as passion was allowed to soar back then.

But I was shy. I never asked her out, not to the Alps Road Drive-in Theater, not even to the Varsity for a double steak sandwich with extra onions and pickles.

I tried my best to speak to her, but nothing would come out. I wanted to whisper to her in class, "Lovely sweater you're wearing today, my dear," but it always hung there in my throat causing me to cough on her.

I wrote love poems to her and sonnets and even a dirty limmerick in a wild, lustful moment. But I never showed them to her. I figured if I did, she would call campus security.

I suppose the real reason I never made any sort of move on the girl of my boyish dreams, however, was that I was realistic.

I was no day at the beach when I was in college, if you

66

know what I mean. The term for individuals such as me in those days was "lizard."

I had short hair and big ears. I wore glasses. I had a large pimple on my nose that struck when I was a sophomore in high school. It didn't go away until I had been married a year and my wife made me go to the doctor and have it surgically removed.

My pants always seemed to be too short when I was in college. That would have come in handy had there been campus floods, I suppose, but all it really managed to do was expose the fact I hadn't yet gotten the word white socks were out.

I never asked the pretty, blond girl who sat next to me out on a date because I was a lizard, and I knew it, and I figured she did, too.

But the point of all this: While I was in the hospital recently I received a get-well card from this very same girl, now a grown woman, of course.

She said some very sweet things in the card. She said she enjoyed reading what I write. She even said she remembered sitting next to me in class. I never thought she even knew I was alive.

I was happy to get the card even though it was twenty years too late. But I also felt a certain amount of remorse. Dang my hesitancy. Dang my timidity. Dang my big ears.

I won't allow it to go any further than the card, of course. She's probably married with kids—and, anyway, they tore down the Alps Road Drive-in Theater.

But let this be a lesson to the young and foolish. Give in to the mad rushes of love! Never hold back when you are filled with the magic of romance! If nothing else works, try a tube of Clearasil!

Lizards need love, too. Take it from one who has been there.

I Always Hated Flowers

MORELAND, GEORGIA—I ALWAYS HATED FLOWERS when I was a kid. My mother, my grandmother and my Aunt Jessie loved flowers, but it was me they always wanted to go out and work in the dang things.

I was a perfectly well-adjusted lad of ten, and I wanted to do perfectly well-adjusted things that lads of ten want to do, such as play ball and make life miserable for my girl cousin.

But, no. Either my mother or my grandmother or my Aunt Jessie would latch onto my ear at least once a day and send me out to hoe around in their flower garden.

"But real men don't work in flowers," I would protest.

"Get out there in those flowers or we'll serve you quiche for supper again," they would volley back.

(Actually, nobody in Moreland had ever heard of quiche back then—and probably few now—but it made a nice line, so I used it anyway. It's called journalistic license.)

I soon moved from disliking flowers to hating them. I would go through the seed catalogs and draw moustaches on pictures of petunias.

My friends gave me a lot of grief about all the time I had to spend working in flowers, too.

"Wanna play ball?" one would ask.

"Him, play ball?" another would scoff. "He's got to work in his mommy's *flowers*."

I tried everything to escape those botanical gardens of hell. I even tried to bribe my girl cousin into doing the work for me. I offered her my best marble, a Johnny Podres baseball card, and not to throw rocks at her anymore if she would do my flower work for me.

"Why don't you sit on a cactus, begonia breath," she countered.

I remember telling my Aunt Jessie, who had by far the greenest thumb in the family, how much I hated flowers.

"When I grow up," I said, "I'll never look at a flower again."

She said I might change my mind one day. I figured she'd been sniffing too many honeysuckle blossoms.

I visited home the other day to see the folks. My grandmother is gone now. My mother is too ill to dabble with her flowers anymore. Aunt Jessie, who has seen a lot of springs, is still out among her gardens every day, however.

First thing I noticed when I drove up my was my aunt's yard. Her azaleas were spectacular, her dogwoods, both pink and white, were in full bloom, and everywhere there were breathtaking blankets of blue and pink thrift.

My mother said people have been driving by from all over the county to witness the blossoming splendor of my Aunt Jessie's yard. I considered swallowing my pride and visiting my aunt next door to tell her how beautiful her yard was and how wrong I had been about flowers.

I didn't though. My old hoe is still out in the garage somewhere, and one word out of me and my Aunt Jessie would have had me back at work faster than a Weedeater can take the fur off a cat's tail.

Flowers or no flowers, if it was hard work I had wanted, I wouldn't have gotten this license to practice journalism in the first place.

My Father Would Have Liked Spring Training

WEST PALM BEACH, FLORIDA—I WISH MY FATHER HAD lived long enough that I could have taken him to a few spring training baseball games.

He would have enjoyed sitting in the glorious south

Florida warmth. He would have worn that big straw hat of
his, and he would have filled the park with his booming
voice, a voice perfect for singing gospel music and berat-
ing umpires.

One of the best things a man can do for his son is pass
along a love for baseball. My father did that for me.

Those summers I spent with him as a child, we roamed
about, looking for whatever it was he was looking for, and
if there was a ball game to see during one of our stops, we
saw it.

We sat swatting mosquitoes on hot south Georgia nights
watching Class D. It was Waycross against Tifton, but an
eight-year-old at a ball game with his dad doesn't care that
Class D is a million miles from Yankee Stadium. They still
hit the ball and run, and the hot dogs taste just as good.

We were in a hotel one night in Nashville and the Little
Rock Travelers were there, too, for a Southern Association
series with the Nashville Vols.

My father walked up to the Little Rock manager in the
lobby and asked for a signed baseball for his son. The
manager located the equipment man and I had my ball. I
still have it.

I have promised myself I will make this annual pilgrim-
age to spring training as long as I am able, financially and
otherwise.

The other afternoon, I saw the inaugural game at the
Houston Astros' new training complex in Kissimmee.
Houston beat the Yankees and an usher made Yankee
owner George Steinbrenner show him his ticket.

Later, I went to Tinker Field in Orlando and caught a
Twins' game. At Tinker Field you can walk down to the
visitors' bullpen and stand a few feet behind the catcher
and see firsthand what a batter sees when he faces major
league pitching.

In Fort Lauderdale I watched my team, the Atlanta
Braves, shut out the Yankees. I hate the Yankees, but their
spring park is nice. There are murals of Babe Ruth on the
walls, and they must import the vendors from New York

for these games. Those vendors, with their trays filled with Pepsi, cry, "Soduh heuh."

After the games, I pass the time with friends—others who refuse to grow up as long as they hold to their passion for baseball.

We talk the game. We dissect the game. We talk of our memories of the game. Women make marvelous companions, but I've yet to meet one who remembers Larry Sherry of the Dodgers was the 1959 World Series' most valuable player.

I'm certain I never thanked my father for introducing baseball into my life. We had far too little time together for such.

But when I'm here, in a ballpark, I draw closer to his memory than at any other time.

Nothing could be more valuable than that.

SPORTS

***

Making Athletes Study

SOONER OR LATER, I KNEW A BUNCH OF SCHOOL-
teachers would decide athletes had to study and become
educated like the other students.

This, of course, is what has happened in Texas—of all
places—where the "no-pass, no-play" rule has gone into
effect. Other states, I am certain, soon will follow Texas's
lead.

I don't think we have thought this thing out. As a matter
of fact, I believe we may be making a terrible mistake in
insisting schoolboy athletes become educated.

There are several reasons I believe this:

1. Students who aren't athletes have enough trouble as it
is. I mean, how many dates can you get off your annual
Science Club project?

About all these students had to look forward to was the
future, when, because of their superior grades, they could
expect to get all the good jobs with IBM while all the dumb
jocks would end up working at dumb jobs.

If we insist athletes learn while in school, then the other
students not only won't have dates, but they also probably
will lose out when the IBM jobs are up for grabs.

Let's face it. If both applicants have the same grades,
who is IBM going to pick, a former all-state quarterback or
some wimp?

2. If we start educating athletes, we could wind up with
a lot more politicians like Jack Kemp.

3. How many athletes are going to continue to play such
games as football if we teach them to think for themselves?

Football is a fun game to watch, but it really can't be
that much fun to play. You run around out there and large
people are trying to knock you down to the ground.

Football players have to learn such uncomfortable tactics

as "playing hurt," and "sucking it up." Plus, you can get a variety of rashes and diseases hanging out in locker rooms.

What intelligent person is going, as the coaches say, "to pay the price?"

Educate our athletes and most of them will quit playing ball and start hanging around playing video games with the other students.

4. Give an athlete a quality education and he might start saying intelligent things to the media. As it is, the media can simply make up quotes for athletes because they always say the same things.

"Well, you know, Skip, you know, God gave me, you know, the talent, you know, to play this game, you know, and if you, you know, need any more information, you know, you know you can, you know, get in touch, you know, with my agent."

5. And speaking of the media, if we quit turning out dumb jocks, where will our TV color come from?

6. Educate today's athletes, and today's coaches, yesterday's jocks, will not be able to communicate with their players anymore.

COACH: "Willoughby, what were you thinking about when you made that play?"

WILLOUGHBY: "Goethe."

7. If "no-pass, no-play" spreads, there won't be any more dumb jock jokes like the one where the teacher asks an offensive guard how many seconds there are in a year, and after some contemplation, he answers: "There are twelve. January second, February second, et cetera."

8. And think of this: If athletes become smart, they will stop accepting the charges when the president calls their locker rooms to congratulate them.

Student Athletes

THE MAN HAS BEEN AROUND FOOTBALL ALL HIS LIFE. He has coached it at every level. I asked him to speak frankly about the current rage to make scholars out of collegiate athletes.

I do not necessarily agree or disagree with his viewpoints. However, I thought anonymity would encourage his frankness:

"You know what's the silliest part of this whole thing? It's all this talk about how many players such-and-such coach has to graduate.

"It's not the coach's job to lead his players around to class. Oh, he can make them run to the stadium steps at six in the morning if they don't go to class, but making certain his players graduate isn't a coach's job.

"A college coach has one job, and that is to win. If a coach doesn't win, then he'll get fired.

"Show me a coach who graduates all his players and goes 1–10 five straight years and I'll show you a coach who's out of a job. They'll can him no matter how many Phi Beta Kappas he's got on his squad.

"There's a lawsuit in Georgia where a University of Georgia teacher said she was fired because she wouldn't give preferential treatment to athletes.

"Hey, most of those kids who got the special treatment were black. They were in a remedial program because that is a way to get minority students who aren't otherwise qualified into college.

"The federal government says those kids deserve a chance, and that's the way you give it to them. Sure, they got preferential treatment. Don't give these kids a chance, don't give them a second chance or maybe even a third, and most

77

of them will wind up back down in the country pumping gas.

"Let me tell you about all those test scores and high school grade-point averages. They don't mean a thing. I had kids at (his last school) who made 400 on the SAT's. You'd figure these kids wouldn't make it anywhere.

"But they did. They did because they had good attitudes, and their attitudes got better when they got out of those terrible high schools, and they began to grow up and see the importance of learning.

"I had a kid who made a 400 and guess where he is now? In medical school. Yeah, he's black, and if he were coming along today, under the new NCAA standards, he wouldn't get a chance at anything.

"There are too many variables to set a standard all high school athletes must meet before they can be signed to a scholarship.

"Not all high schools are the same. Not all kids come from the same backgrounds, the same environment. Those black coaches are right. Raise the standards, and college sports will be lily-white again, at least for a long time to come.

"I say let 'em in school. Put 'em in a remedial program. Teach 'em high school courses again, and if it takes them ten years to get a degree, then that's better than getting no degree at all. If they don't get a degree, maybe they will have at least learned how to fill out an application for a job.

"In a perfect world, a university is only for scholars. In the one we live in, which is imperfect, it ought to be for everybody, for whatever they can get from it."

The Kid Who Could Have Been Somebody

THIS KID HAS EIGHT BROTHERS AND SISTERS. HIS FATHER is dead. His mother finds work where she can, mostly as a domestic.

The family lives cramped in a small, rundown house in a mostly rural county.

Sometimes, the kid shows up at school. Sometimes, he doesn't. School is hard. The teachers talk about things of which he knows nothing. Maybe he would try if he understood what the other kids seem to understand.

He comes home at night and nobody asks, "What did you learn in school today?" His mother is too tired from too many years of walking against the wind to care.

But there is at least one thing that is special about this kid. He is big and he is strong and he can run fast.

His teachers promote him along because they don't think the kid has the ability to learn.

But he can play the game. And when he is playing, only then is he living. He finds he *is* better than others in at least something, and that something is playing the game. Everybody needs a little self-esteem.

He still isn't worth two cents in the classroom. But on Friday nights he owns the world.

Nobody in his family has ever been to college. That's a laugh. Nobody in his family even made it out of high school with a diploma.

But his coaches tell this kid he might have a chance. He might have a chance to get an athletic scholarship. Maybe even to one of the big schools—Oklahoma, Alabama, Ohio State, Georgia.

But there is a problem. This kid is a senior in high school and he can't compose a simple sentence. He reads on a third-grade level.

His grade-point average is a joke. He takes the Scholastic Aptitude Test. He doesn't understand the questions because he can't read them. He doesn't even understand the test monitor's instructions. He bombs.

Perhaps a few years earlier, he might still have been able to go to college and play ball. The National Collegiate Athletic Association had not raised its academic standards for student athletes back then.

But now it takes a 700 on the SAT to be eligible for an

athletic scholarship. This kid couldn't have scored a 700 with two brains.

Before the changes in standards maybe this kid could have accepted this scholarship and have been enrolled in some sort of development studies program where instructors gave him special attention and might have just been able to fill the gaps left by his high school instructors and his home life.

The kid could have played ball. He could have been somebody. And maybe by playing ball, maybe by having his horizons broadened by travel and by being around and learning from his coaches and teammates, he could have been where he could go if he could learn to learn.

Granted, it would have been a long shot, but stranger things have happened.

But what's the use of such conjecture? The NCAA finally got tough on academics and this kid got caught under the steamroller.

Serves him right for being born into a no-win situation.

America Owes Howard Cosell an Apology

AMERICA OWES HOWARD COSELL AN APOLOGY. WE CAN smooth things out with the Egyptians and the Italians later. This can't wait.

Monday Night Football was something special back when Howard was a member of the broadcast team. Millions watched it and planned their weeks around it.

Bars and taverns had special prices on beer on Monday nights and bought oversized TV screens so that no matter how much beer their patrons drank, they could still see the action.

Oversized TV screens also were important because after

the patrons drank too much beer, they would start throwing their glasses at Howard. Very few would have been able to hit the target if it had been a regular sized TV screen.

In American homes, women and children were sent to bed early so as not to interrupt the broadcast with meaningless patter.

The crime rate even went down on Monday nights during football season. There simply was nobody left on the street to mug.

And why? Howard Cosell, that's why. Very few people liked Howard Cosell on *Monday Night Football*, but that's the point.

Americans learned to love to hate Howard, and once he left the broadcast to pretenders, the broadcast became deathly dull.

An acquaintance who runs a drinking establishment said, "Now, Monday nights are no different from any other nights. Our customers still drink a lot of beer, but they throw their glasses at one another instead of at the TV."

I recently read Howard Cosell's new book, *I Never Played the Game*. What we never realized was that Howard's feelings were hurt by all the disdain we showed him.

In the book, he points out that it was he who made *Monday Night Football* in the first place, and he simply got sick and tired of the way he was treated.

So what are we left with now that Cosell's microphone has been silenced?

Frank Gifford to call the action and O. J. Simpson and Joe Namath to make the meaningless patter, that's what.

My regular Monday night reading group canceled its meeting recently, and I, out of curiosity more than anything else, tuned in a *Monday Night Football* broadcast. Chicago was playing Green Bay. Howard would have been great on a game like that:

"Chi-cah-go, Ill-ee-noi, the Windy City, my kind of town, as Ol' Blue Eyes once crooned, is toddling with an excitement tonight unparalleled since the Papa Bear,

George Halas, the father and founder of this sport, forged
from his genius the mighty Monsters of the Midway. . . ."

Instead of that, we got Namath and O.J. talking about
their new baby daughters. Donahue might be interested in
that sort of thing but not a bunch of guys standing around
looking for something at which to throw a glass of beer.

I suppose Cosell has his revenge, though. He's off the
Monday night broadcast and we are left to put up with Giff
and the Football Daddies.

I'd as soon watch wrestling.

Pig Polo

PALM BEACH, FLORIDA—HERE AT THE PLAYGROUND OF
the rich in south Florida, you can pick up a newspaper and
find reports from the polo matches on the front page of the
sports section where baseball ought to be.

Obviously, polo is very important to the well-heeled of
the area who drive out to the matches in their Rollses and
then discuss between chukkers how difficult it is to find
good help these days.

I have never seen a polo match and neither has anyone I
know. A friend of mine, Glenn McCutchen, says he was in
Palm Beach on business once and actually attempted to see a
little polo.

"I read there was going to be a match at the Palm Beach
Polo Club," Glenn reported, "and so I asked somebody at
the front desk at my hotel how to get there.

"He looked over at me, turned up his nose and said,
'I'm sorry, sir, but I am not allowed to divulge such information to anyone from the masses.'"

I didn't make it to the polo matches during my stay in
Palm Beach, either. When I asked at my hotel for directions

to the club, the man behind the desk suggested I go bowling instead.

I was quite discouraged, because the reason I wanted to see a polo match in the first place involved a humanitarian effort on behalf of America's beleaguered farmers.

This all began when I received a letter some time ago from one David S. Burre, who has an engineering firm in Atlanta.

Mr. Burre pointed out that he and a group of his friends were drinking one evening in a place called the High Horse Tavern and came up with a way for farmers to get out of their financial straits.

The idea goes something like this: In every small town and village in America, there should be established a polo franchise.

Because polo ponies are so expensive, Mr. Burre's idea is to have the game played while mounted on pigs.

"Pig polo," said David Burre. "Finally the layman, for a small investment of three hundred fifty dollars, could own a thoroughbred-type animal—a polo pig—and think of the money farmers could make selling pigs to pig polo franchises.

Mr. Burre and his friends, who admittedly birthed his idea after a night of considerable consumption, already have devised rules for pig polo. Here are a few:

—A period is called a "lard."

—No slopping of the pigs between lards.

—No rooting, for the home team or otherwise, allowed.

—Umpires are licensed USDA inspectors.

I think this idea has merit. It's time we helped the farmer and it's time the rest of us—members of the great unwashed—were given the opportunity to enjoy the great sport of polo, even if we have to ride pigs to do it.

I don't know what the spiffy types in Palm Beach do after a polo match is over, but in David Burre's pig polo, the fun has just begun when the final oink is sounded.

In pig polo, you see, the winners get to celebrate by cooking and eating the losers' mounts.

Skiing Can Be Fun

DEER VALLEY, UTAH—SKIING CAN BE A LOT OF FUN. My favorite parts are taking off those heavy boots at the end of the day and getting some feeling back in the hands and feet several hours after I have left the frigid slopes.

But snow skiing does have its annoyances, and people should be made aware of these before they decide to take up the sport and go out and spend a lot of money on equipment and airline tickets to take them to such ski resorts as Deer Valley, which is located in the majestic Wasatch Mountains, fifty minutes from the airport in Salt Lake City where a lot of Mormons live.

As a public service to those who may think they would like to join the growing hordes of snow skiers, I thought I better mention a few of the problems:

LEARNING TO SKI—It is easy to learn to ski. All you do is point your skis downhill and off you go. What is difficult to learn is how to turn on skis and how to stop on skis.

I saw a man ski into a condominium once because he had not learned to turn or stop. He was fine after they turned his head back in the right direction, but the condo owner's wife, who was giving a Tupperware party when the intruder skied into her living room, was never quite the same after the incident.

SKIING CAN BE A HASSLE—The pain-in-the-neck factor in skiing is one of the highest in outdoor sports. You have to carry your skis a lot, and they are heavy and unwieldy.

You have to learn to walk in those boots, which hurt your feet and ankles, and you have to wear long underwear which itches. If you don't like heavy lifting, your feet and ankles hurting, and itching from long underwear, I suggest you forget skiing and take up bowling, where the only bad part is wearing those silly looking red and green shoes.

FALLING—Every skier, no matter how advanced he or she becomes, occasionally will fall into the snow. This can be painful, not to mention humiliating. When you fall, it is best to feign a heart attack so nobody will think you are so unathletic you couldn't find the fingerholes in a bowling ball.

FIFTEEN-YEAR-OLDS—The most dangerous thing on a ski slope is a fifteen-year-old boy going flat out who doesn't care if he gets killed or if he kills somebody else. Nobody has been able to find the abominable snowman because he's hiding from fifteen-year-old boys on skis.

SKI INSTRUCTION—All the male ski instructors look like Greek gods. Your wife and/or girlfriend will spend hours staring at the male ski instructors in those tight ski instructor pants. Female instructors, on the other hand, look weather beaten and are former college field hockey players.

THE MORMONS—The Mormons are in charge of everything in Utah, including the state's liquor laws which are so complex it's easier to drive to Wyoming to pick up a six-pack than it is to stay in Utah and try to figure out which day it's not against the law to order a vodka tonic if you're left-handed.

If you still want to take up skiing after reading this, good luck. If you don't I'm glad I warned you. If you have decided to join the Mormon church, remember Brigham Young didn't ski either.

With all those wives, he didn't have the time.

That Crazy Yankee Owner

IT MAY BE TIME FOR BASEBALL TO DECLARE YANKEE OWNER George Steinbrenner wacko before he hurts somebody, or himself.

Ever seen a guy more squirrelly than George? He has all

that money and owns the world's most prestigious baseball franchise, and he runs it like Duffy's Tavern.

We all know the facts. He hires Manager X and then fires him and brings in Billy Martin, and they fight and argue and scratch for a while, and so Steinbrenner fires Billy Martin and brings in Manager Y.

Manager Y doesn't suit him, so he fires him and brings in Billy Martin again. Repeat all this four times and you've got the Chinese fire drill that George Steinbrenner runs in New York.

I know what some people may be saying. They may be saying, what business is all this of yours? If George Steinbrenner wants to bring in Mr. Ed to manage his ball club, he owns it, so let him do it.

In most instances I would agree, but we're talking about the New York Yankees here, and the New York Yankees are an American tradition.

For decades there have been basically two kinds of people in this country, those who love the Yankees and those who hate them.

I belong to the latter group. I hate the Yankees. I've been hating them thirty years, as a matter of fact.

I have a cousin who was a big Yankee fan when we were growing up. I despised it when he came to my house to visit.

"The Yankees are going great, aren't they?" he would say with that smirk that all Yankee fans had.

"May all your children be born with pinstripes on their bottoms," I would reply.

I've been trying to contact my cousin to get even for all those smirks since Steinbrenner ruined his beloved Yankees, but the coward won't return my calls.

Perhaps Steinbrenner isn't legitimately crazy. Perhaps he simply has a failing memory and forgets he's already tried Billy Martin over and over again when he brings him back every so often to manage the Yankees.

"I would like to announce I am bringing in a bright new kid named Martin to run my team," Steinbrenner tells the press.

"Excuse me," asks a reporter. "Haven't you done this before?"

"I can't remember," answers Steinbrenner.

I realize there are bigger problems in the world than the way George Steinbrenner runs his baseball team.

This is not Reagan's visit to Bitburg nor his trade embargo on Nicaragua.

This isn't the Middle East nor an artificial heart, a network takeover nor even another one of those shuttle shots to space.

But it *is* important to the portion of our society that has built a life around hating the Yankees.

What George Steinbrenner has done is unforgivable. With him at the helm, it's not fun to hate the Yankees anymore.

You just sort of feel sorry for them.

Soccer Is Boring

I DON'T WANT TO SOUND FLIPPANT ABOUT ALL THOSE PEO-ple getting killed in European soccer riots, but I honestly think I know part of the reason for the violence that surrounds the sport in other parts of the world.

It's because soccer is boring to watch. If I had to watch a soccer match or a bowling match, I would take bowling every time.

At least in bowling, you can always laugh at those silly bowling shirts and shoes the bowlers wear. The only thing uglier than a bowling shoe is Gloria Vanderbilt.

Nothing ever happens in one soccer game to set it apart from another. The two teams run up and down the field for a couple of hours and then maybe—just maybe—one of the teams will score a goal.

I can give you the soccer scores for an entire season right here. They will be 0-0, 1-0 or 1-1 most of the time, and occasionally there will be a real slugfest that ends 1 – 1.

What happens in Europe is that all those people get together for a soccer match, and they start drinking and become bored with what's happening on the field, so they riot.

Imagine a riot breaking out in the middle of a close American football game. There is too much head-knocking on the field for such a thing to take place, and since most of the people in the stands have a bet down on the game they aren't going to get involved in a fight because they might have a week's salary wagered on the outcome.

I've never seen a soccer match in person. I avoid soccer matches with the same intensity that I avoid the dentist.

However, I did see a match on television once. I was in London and I turned on the set in my hotel room. The BBC was televising the English soccer version of the Superbowl.

You don't have a lot of choices when it comes to watching the telly in London, so fool that I was, I sat there and watched the soccer match.

The two teams kicked the ball up and down the field for an entire afternoon, but nobody could get the ball past the goalkeepers and the match ended 0 – 0.

No problem. They decided to try again in a couple of days. I found myself in front of my television in my hotel room watching the second stanza of this yawner. I had to see if anybody would ever score.

Late in the second match, somebody kicked the ball and it hit another player in the back of his head and accidentally went into the goal. Team A took the championship 1 – 0. I've seen more excitement at a K mart tire sale.

What the crowds at the two matches did most was sing. There was nothing to watch on the field, so they sang— which of course is better than rioting, but some of the best fights I've ever seen started with a bunch of drunks trying to sing at a bar.

What comes off the top of my head as a means of making soccer more exciting is to give the players baseball bats, and if the match happens to end in a tie then let the respective goalies fight it out in a bare-knuckles tie-breaker.

As we have proved with many of our popular American sports, it is better to have the violence on the field than in the bleachers.

Georgia on Probation

My alma mater, the University of Georgia, has been placed on probation by the National Collegiate Athletic Association (NCAA) for recruiting violations within its basketball program.

Georgia gave a prospect a T-shirt. It is against the NCAA rules to give a prospect anything, even a T-shirt.

Georgia gave a friend of another prospect a ride to a restaurant and then to his hotel.

It also is against NCAA rules to give a friend of a prospect anything, even a four-mile ride.

A T-shirt here, a pair of shoes there, a ride for a prospect's friend, and Georgia's athletic department and the entire school suffer the embarrassment of probation.

"I know the charges were minor," a member of the athletic department told me. "But nobody outside the inner circle really pays attention to the details, so people think we are buying and selling kids like slaveholders."

What was the Georgia coach supposed to do when the prospect's friend asked for a ride? Tell him to walk and probably lose the prospect because he turned his friend out on the street?

We're talking big-time college basketball here, where millions of dollars and extended contracts are on the line. If a tall kid who can dunk with both hands asks for a T-shirt, you give him a T-shirt.

I'm not defending my school here. Georgia knows the rules, yet Georgia broke the rules, as silly as they may be, and Georgia got caught and got punished. And that's the name of that tune.

But the NCAA is like the IRS. They go after you, they get you, with some help from college coaches who turn each other in, some standing on pedestals claiming piously, "We will bring these cheaters to their knees."

Horse dung. They turn each other in for strictly selfish reasons. You get your rival in trouble with the NCAA and the NCAA takes away a few of its scholarships, and all of a sudden you're beating his brains out and you become a genius with a fat raise.

College basketball players are shaving points for gamblers and are going to jail for it. Millions are being handed out for television contracts, big-time coaches are getting rich—and the NCAA is worrying about a high-school kid getting a free T-shirt?

I don't have a solution for all this idiocy, but I know how I wish college basketball and football worked.

Whack Hyber, who coached basketball at Georgia Tech before he got sick of recruiting and quit, had the idea years ago.

"What I would like to be able to do," said Whack, "is to put a sign on the bulletin board in the P.E. department that said, 'Any student desiring to try out for the men's basketball team, report to the gym at four o'clock.'

"I play with the kids who happen to come to my school. You play with the kids who happen to come to yours."

Thus recruiting becomes a thing of the past. The sport purifies itself, and all the athletes get a pair of shoes, socks, a jock and an opportunity to have a little good, clean fun.

MY FRIEND
RIGSBY,
LOVER AND
ENTREPRENEUR

✳ ✳ ✳

New Soft Drink Might Make It

My friend Rigsby, the entrepreneur, called with what he said was a can't-miss idea.

I'm not saying Rigsby often comes up with half-baked ideas that are supposed to make him a fortune and never do, but he's the same guy who tried to start a fast-food franchise that featured burger-on-a-rope.

"What is it this time?" I asked him.

"I'm getting into the soft drink game," he answered.

"What do you know about soft drinks?" I asked again.

"Plenty," he said. "I have an uncle who used to be in soft drinks."

"For real?"

"Sure. He invented a soft drink called '5-Up.'"

"What happened?"

"It flopped, but my uncle didn't give up. He invented another drink and called it '6-Up.'"

"What happened then?"

"It flopped, too."

"What did your uncle do after that?"

"He gave up!"

I cautioned Rigsby that the Coke and Pepsi people just about have the soft drink market cornered.

"You haven't heard my idea," Rigsby said.

"Shoot."

"You know how the soft drink people are into drinks that don't have this or that?" Rigsby asked.

"I mean there's caffeine-free drinks and sugar-free drinks and drinks that don't have saccharin because saccharin kills laboratory mice?"

"Go on," I said.

"Well, my soft drink is going to have it all. We're going to have caffeine and sugar and saccharin and NutraSweet and sodium and MSG, and all that good stuff people miss."

"It won't work," I said. "People are too conscious today regarding what they put inside their bodies."

"Not everybody," said Rigsby.

"What do you mean?"

"There's Mikey in the TV commercials," he went on. "He'll eat anything."

"But who else?"

"People who don't mind taking a risk, that's who," said Rigsby. "There must be people out there who are fed up with all the don't-drink-this's and don't-drink-that's who don't mind taking a risk now and then to get what they want.

"I want people who will walk on the wild side, spit in the devil's eye and say, 'Don't give me no plastic saddle, I want to feel the leather when I ride.'"

I asked Rigsby if he had a name for his new product.

"My uncle named it," said Rigsby. "It's a name he tried years ago that also flopped."

"So what is it?" I asked.

"Dr. Salt," said Rigsby. "You like it?"

I didn't commit myself, but who knows? Maybe Rigsby really has something this time.

A belt of all those things we like that we aren't supposed to enjoy anymore might do us all a world of good.

Get Control of the Clicker

MY FRIEND RIGSBY, THE LOVER, IS PLANNING TO GET married. He asked my advice concerning a prenuptial agreement.

I happen to be an expert on such matters because I learned the hard way. I've had three wives, but no agreements. If my ex-wives and I formed a musical group, we'd be Po' Boy and the Alimonyettes.

I informed Rigsby he most certainly should have a prenuptial arrangement and that he not forget one very important item.

"Make certain you get control of the clicker," I told him.

"The what?"

"The clicker," I went on. "The little remote control deal that changes the channels on the TV."

"Why is that so important?" Rigsby asked me.

"Without the clicker," I said, "a man is nothing. He has no power."

"Explain," said Rigsby.

"In every household," I began, "somebody must be designated—even if it is necessary to use brute force—to be in control of the clicker or else there would be anarchy.

"One person might say, 'I want to watch *Wheel of Fortune*,' and another might say, 'I want to watch a cable movie,' and another, 'I want to watch the wrestling matches.'

"So everybody would go for the clicker and domestic violence would erupt."

"You mean they might hurt each other?" Rigsby asked.

"There was a story in the papers last week about a family in Tumbleweed, Oklahoma," I told him.

"A man and his wife and their two children sat down to watch an evening's television. All four wanted to see a different program, and nobody had official control of the clicker. They all dived at it at once.

"The man suffered severe scratches from his wife's fingernails, and she was bitten on the ankles by one of the children, who got poked in the eye during the melee. The other child got the clicker and ran outside as he was being chased by the rest of the family and was hit head-on by a jogger. All five were treated and released at a local hospital."

"I never realized something like that could happen," Rigsby said.

"It's like this, my friend," I continued. "Your wife wants to watch *The Newlywed Game*, and you want to see three basketball games, a golf tournament and the last thrilling moments of a Charles Bronson movie on HBO where he blows away a small city.

"If you have the clicker, you can switch back and forth and keep up with everything you want to see. If your wife has control, you'll have to sit there and watch while some woman tries to remember what color undershorts her husband wore on their wedding night."

"I see your point," said Rigsby.

It must be wonderful to have a friend like me.

Paging the Girl of Your Dreams

MY FRIEND RIGSBY, THE LOVER, HAS HAD TROUBLE getting dates lately, so he subscribed to one of those singles magazines you can find in all major cities.

They include a classified section in which both men and women—and whatever else is out there these days—advertise themselves for romantic interludes.

"At first," said Rigsby, "I thought this was the greatest thing since room service. You just thumb through the magazine, pick out what you like, and voilà!—the girl of your dreams."

"You sound as though it didn't work out that way," I said to Rigsby.

"The first ad I answered sounded just like the woman I wanted: 'Blond bombshell with keen interest in the arts.'"

"And when you met her?"

"She was blond OK, but she was also four feet eleven

inches tall, weighed two hundred and eighty pounds, with a tattoo on her left cheek that said, 'Born to Raise Hell.'"

"By 'cheek,'" I asked Rigsby, "do you mean . . . ?"

"Let me put it this way," he answered. "The first thing she did when I went to pick her up was moon me."

"What did you do then?"

"I ran."

"No, I mean did you answer any more ads in the magazine?"

"I was determined," said Rigsby. "The next one sounded terrific: 'Tall, sensuous redhead, looking for man who likes to walk on the wild side.'"

"And what happened with her?"

"She was into S&M."

"She beat you with a whip?"

"Worse. She tied me up and made me watch rock music videos. When she went to her bedroom to look for her spurs, I untied myself and got away."

"Surely, you decided not to answer any more ads after that," I said to Rigsby.

"I found one ad that seemed totally harmless," he said.

"What did it say?"

"'Sweet, sensitive schoolteacher wants meaningful, loving relationship with man who will not only love me, but my pets as well.'"

"And?"

"Ever try to get romantic in the same room with two boa constrictors named Arnold and Hazel?"

"But you kept trying?"

"I did. The next girl I called said she was The Girl-Next-Door Type."

"Was she?"

"That was the problem," said Rigsby. "She turned out to be my neighbor, Hilda Weatherwax, who weighs three hundred pounds and has a moustache. Some guy looked at her the wrong way in the laundry room one night and she stuffed him into the Speed Queen. He was in there for four cycles before the fire department came and got him out."

"Surely you stopped answering ads after that," I said.

"I answered one more. It said 'For a good time, call Gladys,' and we hit it off perfectly."

"So singles magazines do work," I said.

"What magazine?" Rigsby said. "I found Gladys's number in the phone booth at the bus station."

Love in the '80s isn't all that different. In a pinch, you still go back to basics.

Pushy Broads, Inc.

MY FRIEND RIGSBY, THE ENTREPRENEUR, HAS AN IDEA for a new business.

"I'm calling it 'Pushy Broads, Inc.,'" he said.

I reminded him of the new sensitivity and that the name of his new company was blatantly sexist.

"Wait until you hear my idea," he explained. "This will be a great help to women everywhere."

"Shoot," I said.

"You know how women are always getting ripped off by auto mechanics?" Rigsby asked.

"A woman takes her car in to be repaired and the service department manager says to himself, 'Here's my chance to pick up a few easy bucks.'

"All that's wrong with the woman's car is her hood ornament is loose, but the service guy, knowing the woman knows diddly about cars, proceeds to tell her, her low-flat, double pump, lolabrid gelator isn't working properly, and just like that, she gets hit with a three-hundred-dollar repair bill for absolutely nothing."

"How would Pushy Broads, Inc., help these women?" I asked Rigsby.

"What I do is hire about five or six really assertive women and teach them the basics of auto mechanics," he said. "You know the kind. They're always talking loud and they wear those big hats.

"If a woman is afraid she might get ripped off by an auto mechanic, she calls Pushy Broads, Inc.

"We assign one of our pushy broads, I mean assertive females, to take the car in for her. When the auto mechanic starts his funny business, our representative says, 'Whoa, Jack. You're not talking to the Junior League here. What's wrong with the car?'

"If he still wants to be cute, then our representative, who is an expert in such matters, makes a terrible scene.

"First, she starts talking real loud and waving her hands and arms around in the air.

"Then she threatens the guy with a lawsuit and picketing by storm troopers from the National Organization of Women. If she really wants to get nasty, she kicks him in the shins with her special Pushy Broads, Inc., steel-toed pumps. Very few auto mechanics could stand up to all that."

I asked Rigsby if there were other areas in which his organization could help women who are being exploited by the system.

"Let's say a woman is being sexually harassed by her boss," Rigsby explained.

"She calls us and we put one of our girls on her case. Our girl goes to the woman's office and asks the receptionist to see the boss. When the receptionist asks what the nature of her business is, she replies, in a loud voice so everybody else in the office can hear, 'It's about a paternity suit.'

"When she gets in to see the boss, she tells him if he doesn't stop picking on our client, she is going to tell Phil Donahue on him. Just like that our client's problems are over."

Knowing Rigsby always has an alternative plan in case of failure, I asked him what he would do with his girls if Pushy Broads, Inc., didn't work.

"Either I would start a roller-derby franchise or go into the mud-wrestling game," he said. "I would never leave my girls out in the cold."

If every man were as sensitive about women as Rigsby, the gender gap would have never occurred.

MODERN LIFE

✻✻✻

Difference Between Garbage and Trash

DID YOU KNOW THERE WAS A DIFFERENCE BETWEEN trash and garbage?

I'm nearly forty years old, and I didn't know that. I always figured trash and garbage were the same thing, a bunch of stuff you wanted to throw away.

You live, you learn.

The other morning I walked outside my house and noticed the can in which I dump my refuse (a highbrow word for a bunch of stuff you want to throw away) was still full from the previous day.

There was a little note stuck to the can. It said, in essence, that my refuse hadn't been picked up because—and I quote—"trash and garbage had been mixed."

I hate making mistakes like that. I didn't close the cover on a book of matches before striking. It was three weeks before I got over the guilt.

I called Georgia Waste Systems, where I have my trash-garbage account, to apologize. They were very nice and said a lot of people make the same mistake I did and they were not planning a lawsuit.

As long as I had somebody on the phone who could explain, I asked, "What is the difference between trash and garbage?"

"Garbage," said a spokesindividual, "are things that come from the bathroom or kitchen."

"You mean like bread you leave out for a couple of months and green things start growing on it?" I asked.

"Precisely," she said.

"Trash," she continued, "is basically anything else. We do not pick up leaves, for instance, or old furniture, or boxes of materials that were collected when somebody cleaned out their attic."

The lady said it was up to the individual garbage collectors to decide if there is, in fact, trash and garbage mixed on their appointed rounds.

Somehow, I can't visualize two guys on a garbage truck really spending that much time trying to figure out which is which.

"What is it you have there, Leonard? Is it trash or garbage?" one guy says to the other.

"I can't be absolutely certain, Elvin, but it has green things growing on it."

I will, of course, comply with the waste company's dictum against mixing my trash and my garbage, but don't we have enough complexities in our lives as it is?

Don't we have to deal with international terrorism and the women's movement? Don't we have to battle traffic, computer involvement in our lives and airplanes that never take off on time?

Isn't it enough of a burden that we have to decide what to do about Central America, which long-distance telephone company we want to serve us and which cereal has the most fiber?

Oh, for a simpler time, when the good guys won, a girl could still cook and still would, and trash and garbage were the same, both delicacies as far as a goat was concerned.

It is a wonder that more of us don't tie a Glad bag around our heads and tell modern living to go stick its head in the nearest dumpster.

Ban These Commercials

MY CAR RADIO WAS PLAYING MUSIC. THEN, THE MUSIC stopped and a commercial began. A woman was talking about her various problems with constipation. She went into great detail.

I'm not certain why this occurrence caught my attention. People have been talking about all sorts of personal matters on radio and television for years.

But this one time I said to myself: "Here I am riding around in my car on a beautiful summer day, listening to music, and all of a sudden, I've got to hear a play-by-play account of some unnamed woman's problems with her bowels."

Couldn't we, the viewers and the listeners, be spared such?

One, I don't care if the woman has been constipated since the Eisenhower administration. That's her problem and she ought not to be on radio blabbing about it to perfect strangers like me.

Two, where did they find this woman? And how much money did they have to give her to go on the radio and talk about such a personal matter? That's the sort of thing I would try to keep quiet, if it were me.

I called a friend of mine in the advertising game and asked him the questions I had earlier asked myself.

"The woman most likely was a professional, who was just hired to read the script," he explained.

"You mean," I asked, "this was all a ruse? The woman likely does not have the problem she was discussing?"

"I can't say that for sure, of course," he went on, "but people are hired to do commercials just like people are hired to do anything else. She probably got just a standard talent fee for her work."

That's got to be a great way to get into show business.

"Well, how's the career going, Mary Ann?"

"Terrific. Last week I did a laxative commercial."

Then, I suppose, on to bigger things like hemorrhoids and the heartbreak of psoriasis.

There simply are some products that should not be advertised on radio and television.

They also should not be mentioned in a family newspaper, quite frankly, but when one is on a crusade, one must be given certain licenses.

Here is a list of some of the products I would like to see banned from being advertised on radio and television.

HEMORRHOID TREATMENTS—Your doctor can tell you exactly what you need for that problem. So can former president Jimmy Carter and baseball star George Brett, for that matter.

LAXATIVES—We've been over that already.

TOILET BOWL CLEANERS—Please, I'm trying to eat a sandwich here.

DANDRUFF TREATMENTS—Dandruff is gross. I don't want to watch some guy with a dandruff blizzard on his sports jacket get turned down for a job because he hasn't got enough sense to wear white in public.

FEMININE HYGIENE PRODUCTS—Tell Cathy Rigby to go balance on a beam or something and leave the rest of us alone.

STOMACH RELIEF PRODUCTS—Frankly, I don't care how some dock worker spells "relief" when he's got gas. He ought to have the decency to go on home when that happens, anyway.

There are others, of course, but you get the idea. "Diarrhea is no fun in the rain," the man says on the commercial.

It's no fun anywhere that I know of, and I simply don't want to be reminded of that fact.

Car Dealer Commercials

IT SHOULD BE AGAINST THE LAW FOR AUTOMOBILE dealers to do their own television or radio commercials. If they do, then the penalty should be somebody sticks a hot exhaust pipe . . . well, they should be severely punished.

This isn't some half-baked idea I just thought up. This idea is fully baked and it comes from years of listening to car dealers doing their own television and radio commercials.

What is it with these people? Do they think we're deaf?

"NOBODY WILL MAKE YOU A DEAL LIKE CUZZIN TOM AT CUZZIN TOM'S CHIVEY, LOCATED JUST FOUR MILES PAST CUZZIN TOM'S LOAN COMPANY ON CUZZIN TOM BOULEVARD!" Cuzzin Tom will pick you cleaner than buzzards on a dead possum on the highway, and he will spend every decibel in his power to lure you into his trap.

I don't begrudge a guy trying to move a car or two, but why must these money changers go on radio and television and make absolute fools of themselves?

There are several ways car dealers make fools of themselves on radio and television.

There is the patriot: "We sell only American cars, cuz we believe in Americah. If you don't buy a car from us, then you must be some kind of Commanist."

Then there is the I-Am-Just-One-Of-The-Family routine: "We luv you, and we luv yo' chillun and we luv all chillun and we luv evahbody's chillun, and if you buy a car from somebody else, it must mean you one of them chileabusahs. We offer easy financin' right on our lot."

There are the car dealers who recently underwent a frontal lobotomy.

"We've gone crazy at Crazy Al's! We'll sell you any car or truck on our lot at crazy prices! We'll give you a car or truck! We will pay you to take one! Take our cars! Take our trucks! We don't care! We've gone crazy!"

The all-time car dealer who does his own commercials, I firmly believe, is Charles Hardy, and he operates out of Dallas, Georgia.

I'm not sure how many car dealerships Charles Hardy must own, but if it's got wheels, Charles Hardy sells it.

Charles Hardy says, "We luv you and we need you."

Charles Hardy says, ". . . and for goodness sakes, let's take care of those precious chilluns."

Charles Hardy loves America. Charles Hardy is a family

man. Charles Hardy is a country boy who wouldn't slick you.

If you buy a car from Charles Hardy, he will be so appreciative, he'll probably come over to your house once a month to wax it.

And one more thing. I have every right to say these things, because I come from a long line of used car dealers.

Charles Hardy may be all that and he may do all that, but his commercials are driving me crazier than Crazy Al.

There is only one way to stop these people and that is to make it unlawful for them to clutter the airways with their nauseous hard sell.

And if they disobey, I'll tell you where to stick that hot exhaust pipe.

Right up their Isuzus.

A Speed Demon's Auto-Biography

FROM WHAT I READ AND HEAR, IT APPEARS THE NATION may soon get its old speed limit back, or at least one that enables motorists to drive—legally that is—faster than the present snail's pace of 55 miles per hour.

Regardless of what happens to the speed limit, however, I remain convinced it was a good thing my old friend Raymond (Double-clutch) Norsworthy never lived to see the federal government demand a speed limit of 55.

Raymond couldn't have handled it. Speed was his life, his car, his mistress. Trying to slow him down to 55 would have been like taking away Picasso's brush, Van Cliburn's piano, or Jack Nicklaus's putter.

The day Raymond turned sixteen and got his driver's

license was the happiest day of his life. It was also the day his parents tried to do away with him.

For his birthday, his parents gave him a souped-up, '55 Thunderbird, knowing their son immediately would drive it as fast as it would go and probably kill himself.

The Norsworthys, Betty Jean and Frank, had had it in for Raymond ever since he was eleven, when he put his little brother, Arnold, into a dryer down at the laundromat and dropped in a dime.

Little Arnold, who was four at the time, lived through the experience, but it was weeks before they could remove all the lint from the various orifices of his body.

Raymond defied the odds, however, and managed to live several years driving at top speed at all times.

When he arrived at school each morning, the entire faculty and student body would gather outside to see if Raymond could get his T-Bird stopped from the 120 he was doing when he pulled into the parking lot.

Most of the time, Raymond made it. Occasionally, however, he didn't. One morning he drove through the door to the school cafeteria and his car came to a halt only when approximately a hundred pounds of rice pudding clogged his carburetor.

Raymond also continued to terrorize little Arnold, once tying him naked to the T-Bird and using him as a hood ornament.

Raymond also continued to be stopped often by the police. He was driving through a nearby small town one evening and was stopped for speeding.

"How much is the fine?" he asked the officer.

"Ten dollars," was the answer.

Raymond handed the policeman a twenty and said, "Keep the change. I'll be back through here in a couple of hours."

I think of Raymond often, especially now that Americans likely will soon be able to drive faster.

As you probably guessed, Raymond finally did get it in an automobile accident.

He was walking back to his car after buying a new set of foam rubber dice to hang on his rear-view mirror and a woman attempting to parallel-park backed over him.

The blind girl sang Raymond's favorite song, the immortal "Dead Skunk in the Middle of the Road" at his funeral, and little Arnold delivered the eulogy, entitled, "The day my big brother went to that great speedway in the sky, I got my first decent night's sleep in years."

There wasn't a dry eye in the church.

Too Old to Drink?

IF THE FEDERAL GOVERNMENT REALLY WANTS TO FOOL around with the drinking age, it should start at the other end.

What I mean by this is that the government should first do something about older drinkers before it starts meddling with the younger ones.

There are several reasons I think this:

1. Older people can drink a lot more than younger people because they've had more practice.

2. Also, they can afford more to drink. It's tough to get all that drunk when you're on a six-pack-a-week budget.

3. Older people have a lot more reason to drink than younger people. I drink more now than I did when I was twenty. That's because when I was twenty I hadn't been through three divorces and the Nixon presidency.

4. Older people are sloppier drunks than younger people. When older people get drunk, they do things like cry, call their ex-wives in Montana and sit around piano bars making fools of themselves trying to sing "Melancholy Baby."

Young people, on the other hand, get sick when they drink too much. A few beers later they throw up and go to bed while their elders are still out crying, calling their ex-wives in Montana and sitting around piano bars making fools of themselves trying to sing "Melancholy Baby."

As we all know by now, the government has blackmailed the states into raising their legal drinking age to twenty-one. Otherwise, the states would face a loss of federal highway funds.

Fine, but how old should a person be before the government mandates he or she must *quit* drinking and no longer be an embarrassment in public or be a threat to do something stupid like driving while plastered?

Thirty? No. Most thirty-year-olds still have no idea what they are going to do with their lives and need a drink every now and then to convince themselves that one day they, too, will own a Porsche.

Thirty-five? That's still too young. By the time a person is thirty-five, he or she has the Porsche and needs to drink to escape the anxiety of wondering from whence the next payment will come.

Forty? Heavens, no, and there's a good reason for that. I'll be forty in a couple of weeks. I hate to think I had to face that occurrence without the benefit of a few cocktails.

So, how about forty-five? Or fifty? Or fifty-five? Stop me anytime here. Sixty? Seventy. Why don't we simply pick a number at random and say: OK, you're sixty-one (a number at random) and no more booze for you.

Unfair? We did that to young people, didn't we? We picked what sounded like a good number, twenty-one, and we said: Don't care if you're married, a parent, a soldier, whatever. Be twenty-one or be gone.

You know what practically every kid says at least a million times? "It's not fair," that's what they say.

And, sometimes, they're right.

The Medium Is the Message

CONDOMS.

OK, now that I have everyone's attention, let me say that if the mention of that particular product embarrasses or infuriates you, you are going to be embarrassed and infuriated a great deal in the future. Get ready for "The Return of the Condom."

Condoms, long obsolete as a means of preventing disease and pregnancy with the development of penicillin and the pill, began their comeback alongside the rise and awareness of AIDS and teen pregnancy.

Several months ago, one company even began advertising condoms on billboards in certain American cities. I got phone calls and letters.

"How dare they put something like that on billboards," was the prevalent theme of the calls and letters.

That is nothing compared to what is about to happen. In its November issue, *Fortune* magazine featured a detailed study of the sudden surge of condom sales.

Consider this:

—Said New York's health commissioner, at a conference dealing with the threat of AIDS to heterosexuals, "The day of the condom has returned."

—The National Academy of Sciences is advising the use of condoms.

—The surgeon general has endorsed the use of condoms.

—Condom sales are currently up 10 percent and they are expected to climb even higher. And you can expect more ad campaigns.

—Women account for 50 percent of condom sales. One

company's expected to target women with billboards featuring a woman saying, "I like sex. But I don't want to die from it."

Also, according to *Fortune*, there will be seven days of on-campus festivities at a number of colleges and universities as a means of heightening the awareness of condoms in students. Call it National Condom Week.

According to *Fortune*, "In addition to tossing water-filled condoms around, the events will include the distribution of free condoms, condom motif T-shirts and posters . . . and free condom-promoting literature."

A pin-the-condom-on-the-man contest mirrors pin-the-tail-on-the-donkey with obvious differences.

One of the schools where such is supposed to take place is strait-laced Methodist Emory University in Atlanta. Said Gerald Lowrey, associate dean of campus life at Emory: "Our students can do something independently if they want to, but the school can't be involved in something like this. It just wouldn't do for our reputation. It's too sensational."

But isn't it important for Emory students to be aware of condoms as a means to protect themselves from deadly disease and pregnancy?

"Done right," Lowrey continued, "it's a good thing to get the message out, but the main intent of these campus activities seems to hold the idea up to public ridicule rather than the sensible approach."

The use of condoms might very well save a lot of lives in the future, so any methods of making people use them seem sensible enough to me.

National Condom Week. It begins on Valentine's Day.

A Moment of Silence

When the Supreme Court ruled against an Alabama law that calls for a moment of silence in classrooms so the students can pray if they wish, here came the zealots again with their cries of "The heathens win another one."

When will this silly debate over prayer in schools ever end? I notice there are few students involved in all this. They're too busy trying to make heads or tails out of their algebra lessons.

No, it's the adults who are waging this war. Why do adults always get in the middle of something the kids probably could solve a lot more peacefully if left on their own?

The debate over prayer in the schools is dumb. The Constitution states quite clearly there is to be separation of church and state in this country.

School is state. Prayer is church. End of argument, as far as I'm concerned.

Besides, if you mix the two, you're messing with the Constitution, and you don't mess with Charles Bronson, Mother Nature or the Constitution. Sooner or later, they will all get revenge.

OK, so there are parents out there reading this and they are devout people and they want their children to be devout and they are asking, if my kid isn't allowed to pray at school will he or she grow up to be an atheist?

Of course not. Let's say we finally end this fracas, and we remove all semblance of religion from our public schools.

No problem. Tell your kid to pray before he or she goes to school.

"Dear God, please get me through one more day of algebra."

Or tell your child to pray when he or she gets home from school.

"Dear God, thank you for letting me get through one more day of algebra."

Nobody, not even the Supreme Court, can stop your child from praying in school, for that matter. All your child has to do is tune out for a couple of seconds and say a private, little silent prayer.

"Dear God, please don't let the algebra teacher call on me."

I've always thought God probably listens more closely to silent, individual prayers anyway.

Anybody can stand up with a group of others and recite a prayer. We used to do that when I was in school. Each morning, we would all stand and bow our heads and close our eyes and recite the Lord's Prayer.

One morning, I noticed Alvin Bates, the class jerk, didn't have his eyes closed during the prayer, and when it was over, I said, "Teacher, Alvin Bates didn't have his eyes closed during the prayer."

"If you had your eyes closed," said the teacher, "how do you know Alvin had his open?"

One thing I never liked about teachers is they browbeat you with logic.

But speaking of teachers, the only people who suffered any real injury from the Supreme Court ruling may have been them.

For the heck of it, I talked to an Alabama teacher and asked what she thought of losing the moment of silence in her classroom.

"I'll miss it," she said. "It was the only relief I got from those chatterboxes all day."

My Son Is Wearing an Earring

A MAN WHO IDENTIFIED HIMSELF AS THE FATHER OF A sixteen-year-old son phoned me asking for my advice.

"My son," said the man, "came home the other day wearing an earring."

There was a break in his voice. He obviously was holding back tears.

"What," he said after regaining his composure, "should I do about it?"

I asked the man if he suspicioned his son might be gay.

"That thought did cross my mind," he said, "but my son is currently dating three members of the school's cheering squad and an entire shift of waitressess at Burger King."

I asked the man if his son was a member of any sort of musical group. Young musicians have a tendency toward odd behavior and strange dress, such as thrashing about on stage as if they were having some sort of fit and styling their hair with a Weedeater, not to mention wearing earrings.

"We knew he had no musical talent or interest," replied the father, "when they gave him a tambourine to play in the third grade rhythm band and he asked the teacher where he was supposed to blow into it."

I told the man I had no children of my own but I had regularly watched *Leave It to Beaver*, had witnessed Beaver's dad, Mr. Cleaver, solve many child-rearing crises and that I would offer any advice I could regarding his particular problem.

Even if the young man isn't gay or isn't a member of any musical group, there remain several other possible reasons why he suddenly would decide to wear an earring and heap embarrassment upon his father and cause the poor man to wonder where he had gone wrong.

The father might want to check and make certain his son isn't wearing undershorts that are too tight. Undershorts that are too tight often are the cause of many maladies, such as migraine headaches, disco fever and possibly even a sudden desire to adorn one's earlobe.

The boy may be eating too much junk food, too. Such a diet can be the source of many problems in youngsters, such as terminal acne, sullenness, wearing one glove for no apparent reason and possibly even the earring bit, too.

What I really suspect, however, is that the man's son has fallen in with the wrong crowd at school, a group of obnoxious little punks who have become a bad influence on him, like Eddie Haskell was to Wally and the Beaver.

What the man should do is make certain his son doesn't hang out with such riffraff who enjoy making their parents' lives miserable and then pop the kid on top of his head a couple of times and while he's still dizzy from the blows, pull that stupid earring out of his ear and flush it down the toilet.

I have no doubt that Ward Cleaver would have done the very same thing if one of his sons had tried to break his heart.

Are You Listening, Daddy?

I HAPPENED TO BE IN A GATHERING OF ALL MALES RE-cently, and I don't remember how the subject came up, but a man said, "I'm just glad my daddy didn't live long enough to see me getting my hair cut in a beauty parlor."

I immediately thought of my own father, who died before I stopped getting my hair cut and started getting "styled."

I used to go to Grover's Barber Shop. Now, I have followed other modern men, and I get my hair shampooed, conditioned and styled at a place called "Blowout."

Melissa does my hair. Quite often, there are ladies on each side of me having their hair done, too. That's all the place needs to be a bona fide beauty parlor.

I had become fairly comfortable in that setting, but after what the man said about his father, I somehow felt I had betrayed my own.

My father was a military man. He was wearing a crew-cut the day I was born, and he was wearing one the day he died.

I have to temper this story a bit for a family newspaper, but a man who served in the army with my father told this:

"We had some new recruits in around '54, and the captain (my father) had them standing at attention.

"He went down the row, asking each recruit where he was from, and he came to a kid with what was considered long hair back then.

"The captain said, 'Soldier, how long has your hair been in that condition?'

"The kid replied, 'Since I started high school, sir.'

118

"The captain said, 'I want you to report to the post physician right away. Do you understand?'

"The kid said, 'Yes, sir, but what do I do when I get there?' The captain replied, 'Ask him to give you a complete physical to verify whether or not you're in the wrong outfit and need to be transferred to the WACS.'"

My hair is not that long by today's standards, but if Daddy could see me now, I am certain he would be shocked.

I can hear him now: "In the name of God, son, Liberace doesn't have that much hair."

My father considered Liberace to be the epitome of the lowest form of male life.

There are a number of things I do today that would shock my father were he still alive.

Besides the hair on my head, I have a moustache and a beard.

"Only movie stars and homosexuals have beards," he likely would say, "and I haven't seen any of your movies lately."

I play golf. He abhorred golf.

"Silly game," he'd say. "Hit the ball and then go find it."

I don't wear socks very often. After my father left the army, he became a teacher. I saw him send two tenth-graders home during a basketball game, telling them not to return until they were wearing "the proper footwear."

And I get my hair cut in a beauty parlor. If you're listening, Daddy, forgive me.

And consider this: At least I don't use hair spray.

Why Not Toss a Coin?

A NUMBER OF THINGS BOTHER ME ABOUT THE IRAN-IRAQ war.

First, did Iran invade Iraq or did Iraq invade Iran? And, is it the Iraq-Iran war, or the Iran-Iraq war? Do we have the basis for rock lyrics here: "Did Iran invade Iraq/or did Iraq invade Iran?/Iraq-Iran, Iran-Iraq/Iraq around the clock/Stay and be my lovin' man."

Secondly, I never know what to believe when I read about the war.

One day, the headlines read, "Iraq claims 7 zillion Iranians killed in a desert battle."

The next day, I get, "Iran says nobody left in Iraq but dogs and camels."

For all we really know, there might not be a war going on at all. This could be just some public relations firm's way of introducing a new line of desert tents.

What else bothers me is that I'm not certain who to pull for in the war.

Would the United States benefit more if Iran won, or if Iraq won? How would the war's outcome affect my winter heating bill and gasoline prices? Which side has the best looking uniforms? (I often use that to determine who I'd prefer in a sporting contest, which is why I never pull for the Houston Astros, whose uniforms look like they were patterned after a dish of orange marmalade.)

If Iran wipes out a few million Iraqis (Irocks, Iraqanians, Iraqonians) should I sleep a little better at night, or vice versa?

Just off the top of my head, I'd say I should pull for Iraq. The Iranians took Americans hostage; the ayatollah, who looks like Gabby Hayes with a bad case of constipation, has given our last two presidents that same condition; and two of its leading exports are hatred and terrorism. But Iraq's not exactly a bastion of freedom and good will to all, either. If Iran is John Dillinger, Iraq is at least Pretty Boy Floyd.

I interviewed some other Americans to see which side they favored.

Tossing out those who hadn't heard about the war, didn't have an opinion, were drunk, who thought I was a member of some strange religious sect, who were busy writing Oral Roberts a check, and who were blowing bubbles with their saliva when they were asked, the results were too close to call.

One man did put the matter in its proper perspective, however.

"It's like asking to pick between cancer and AIDS," he said.

Perhaps what we all have here is the same position the late Georgian, Bill Munday, pioneer sportscaster, found himself in one evening before he was to broadcast the Yale-Harvard football game. "Who do you prefer in tomorrow's game?" a Harvard student asked him, "Yale or fair Harvard?"

"Neither one," he said. "You're all a bunch of damn Yankees and I hope you both lose."

Koko, the Talking Gorilla

WE ARE OFTEN WARNED NOT TO BELIEVE EVERYTHING we read in the newspaper.

Since I work for one and understand a journalist's eternal search for truth, however, I have rarely doubted any information provided me in newsprint.

But now this:

There was a wire service article that ran the other day concerning a talking gorilla named Koko.

The story was out of something called the Gorilla Institute in Woodside, California, and it was all about this alleged gorilla that had a thing for cats.

The gorilla, a female, had a cat and she played with it and held it and wrapped blankets around it and apparently loved it as her own.

The cat died last Christmas, however, the story went on to say. Koko now has a new cat and has stopped grieving over the one that died.

After her cat died, Koko, according to the story, said things like "frown" and "sad" and asked for another cat by saying, "Tiger, please."

I don't have any problems with the gorilla liking the cat. Often there are instances of different kinds of animals taking up with one another. We had a chicken at home that was quite fond of our dog, for example.

Whenever I went out to play with my dog, Arnold, the chicken would join us and run after balls just like Arnold. The chicken loved Arnold, as a matter of fact, and would fly upon Arnold's back and ride with him wherever he went.

Unfortunately for both Arnold and the chicken, Arnold was always chasing cars.

One day, he caught one with the chicken on his back. I buried them side by side under the big oak tree.

But I'm getting away from the original idea here. What I doubted about the gorilla story was the report Koko could talk.

Well, not really talk, as in opening her mouth and pronouncing words. But she has been reported to have a vocabulary of five hundred words, which she expresses by sign language.

My problem with such reports about animals being able to communicate with people is the animals never say what you figure an animal would say if it really could talk.

I mean if Koko really can speak her mind, why doesn't she say, "Let me out of here!"

You think any sensible gorilla would really enjoy being penned up in a cage and being made to do all sorts of tiresome things like learning sign language?

Heck no. If I were a gorilla, I would want to be back in the jungle hanging out with my pals and eating bananas in a tree, and if I could talk I would say so.

And then there's the new cat they gave Koko. What does the cat have to say about all of this? You think a cat wants to be in a cage with a large gorilla who thinks it's her baby?

If I were the cat, I know what I would say. I'd say, "Hold it, Jack, I'm not being 'nursemaided' by no gorilla."

All this makes me wonder what Arnold would have said about that chicken if he could have talked.

Probably, "Get that stupid chicken off my back before I go ape."

Standing in Line

WHY IS IT THAT WHENEVER YOU HAVE TO DEAL WITH any branch of any level of government it always is necessary to stand in line?

Did the founding fathers have anything to do with this? Did Ben Franklin figure if Americans had to stand in line before dealing with the government then Americans would avoid dealing with the government at all costs, and government workers would have more time to do a better job?

I've stood in all kinds of lines when dealing with my government. When I was eighteen and there still was a draft, I had to stand in line in order to register.

I had to wait so long, by the time I got to the end of the line I was already three days past my eighteenth birthday, and the barracuda who was registering the nation's young men said, "If I had my way about it, I'd draft you right now."

You're standing in line one minute and you're fighting in service for your country the next.

If they had sent more people like that old bat down at the draft board to Vietnam, there wouldn't have been any need for me to register in the first place.

I've stood in line to get my auto tag. I've stood in line to get a copy of my birth certificate. I've stood in line to get a passport, to obtain various marriage licenses and to pay various fines.

Most recently, I had to stand in line to get my driver's license renewed, but that is only part of the story.

Several days after I stood in line to get my license renewed, I received a letter advising me that the driver's license people had fouled up and had put the wrong Social Security number on my new license.

The letter was very apologetic, and, as I read it, I expected to see, "We'll drop by your house at your earliest convenience in order to clear up our mistake."

Wrong.

What the letter said was that I had to return to the driver's license place again in order to clear up *their* error.

Once again there was a line. I said to myself, "Surely, they won't make me stand in line again. After all, this wasn't my fault."

There was a woman sitting at a desk. I handed her the letter and explained my predicament.

"Just go to the back of the line," she said, "and wait your turn."

Is this what this country is all about? Did Paul Revere make his midnight ride, did John Paul Jones continue to fight, did Teddy Roosevelt and his Rough Riders charge up San Juan Hill in order to preserve our way of life just so we would all have to stand in line to get our driver's license when it wasn't our fault we didn't get the license the first time?

I had no choice but to stand in the stupid line again. They had done the same thing to a woman standing in front of me.

"They can't do this to us!" I said to the woman. "We should write our congressman about this outrage!"

"I thought the same thing," replied the woman, "until I saw the line to buy stamps at the post office."

Colonel Khadafy—The No. 1 El Freako

THROUGHOUT HISTORY THERE ALWAYS HAS BEEN AT least one nut case loose who is trying to play havoc with the rest of the world.

There was Attila the Hun, of course. Great guy when you got to know him, said his best friend, Leroy the Hun, but he was bad to sack cities and rape and pillage.

(The term "rape" I am familiar with, but I've never quite known what you do when you sack a city or pillage whatever it is you pillage. I slept through most of the ancient history courses I had in high school.)

In more modern times we have had Hitler, Idi Amin and the Duvalier boys from Haiti.

But the No. 1 el freako in the world today has to be Colonel Muammar Khadafy of Libya, who is so nutty he spells his last name six or seven different ways.

I'm not certain what it is Colonel Khadafy wants. Attila the Hun wanted to rape, sack and pillage. Hitler wanted to rule the world. Colonel Khadafy apparently wants to be a large pain in the world's behind. (I'm not certain where the world's behind is, but Libya certainly would be one of my first guesses. New Jersey wouldn't come until much later.)

If that is what Colonel Nutso wants, he is doing a very good job of getting it. He's in the papers most days, he's on the tube most every night, and he has gotten so much attention as the world's bad boy he has become a household word. Like "toilet."

I have observations about how we should handle the colonel and the Libyan situation.

First, I think we should launch an investigation into the

fact that Colonel Khadafy looks very much like the baseball pitcher Joaquin Andujar. We all know this from watching the World Series last year in which Andujar, then with the St. Louis Cardinals, set a World Series record for throwing temper tantrums à la Khadafy, not to mention bean balls.

Could it be that Joaquin Andujar and Colonel Khadafy are the same person? Have you ever seen them photographed together? If they are the same person, then all we have to do is get a few marines to hide in the opposing team's dugout one night. When Andujar-Khadafy walks in, the marines could beat him with fungo bats until he promises to go back to Libya and shut up.

Also, we could send him a year's supply of Tylenol, or spread a rumor he has AIDS. We could send Frank Borman to run his personal finances, or we could get Dr. Jan Kemp to sue him.

I heard Senator Howard Baker of Tennessee, who might even become our next president, make a speech recently. He told a joke that isn't a bad idea of how to handle Khadafy, either.

"One morning," Senator Baker began, "President Reagan called his aides and wanted them to bring John Hinckley, who tried to assassinate him, to the Oval Office.

"When Hinckley arrived, the president said he had forgiven him and would order his release.

"Hinckley was overwhelmed. He said, 'Thank you, Mr. President. Is there anything I could do to repay you for your kindness?'

"The president said, 'Well, there is this one little thing.' He took a folder out of his desk and pulled out a picture of Colonel Khadafy.

"He said to Hinckley, 'See this guy? He's dating Jodie Foster . . .'"

What's Going on with Senior Proms?

An Atlanta father whose daughter is graduating from high school this year called and asked, 'Do you know what's going on with senior proms?"

I confessed I didn't. The last time I thought about a senior prom was twenty-one years ago.

"A lot of things have changed since you and I were that age," the father said.

I asked for specifics.

"First, you wouldn't believe how much some girls are paying for the dresses to wear to their proms. My daughter has classmates who are spending up to three and four hundred dollars.

"Most of the boys rent their formals, but they still have to buy their dates flowers, and many parents fork over the money to their sons to rent limousines."

Kids today are taking limos to their senior proms?

"It's because of all this concern about drunk driving. Parents had rather rent their kids a limo and not have to worry about them being in a wreck or getting thrown in jail for driving under the influence."

I said that sounded like sound thinking to me, but why don't they simply drive their kids to the prom and then pick them up when it is over, thus solving the drunk-driving thing and saving the money they would have to spend on a limo?

"I asked my own daughter the same thing," the father replied, "and she said any kid whose parents drove them to the prom would be the laughingstock of the school."

It's been a long time and I suppose I have forgotten how tough peer pressure can be on a teenager.

"You haven't heard it all," the father said. "I know one group of parents who chartered a bus for their kids and put a bar and bartender on the bus so the kids could ride from party to party without having to worry about getting stopped by the cops.

"A lot of proms are at hotels. Some parents are even renting hotel rooms for their kids, so they won't be out driving drunk.

"The hotels make the parents come down and pay in advance and give permission for their children to stay in the rooms.

"I'm sure the parents know that their kids wind up sleeping with their dates, but again they say it's better to have them in bed with their dates than in a car with them."

I asked the man if he allowed his daughter to take part in any of this.

"No," he said, "and she says she'll never speak to me again."

What appears to be happening here is today's high school students are no dummies and they are holding the drunk-driving hysteria over their parents' heads in order to get to do a lot of fun things like riding in limos and shacking up with their dates.

I'm not a parent so don't look for any answers from me, but I do know what my own mother would have said to me if I had said to her, "Mom, I need money for a limo to the senior prom and for a hotel room or else I might get drunk and drive."

She would have said, "Have your butt home at a decent hour and if I find out you've been drinking, I'll tan your hide."

Parents apparently were better at explaining things back then than they are today.

Modernizing Monopoly

I RAN INTO MY FRIEND RIGSBY COMING OUT OF A DEPART-
ment store. He had been buying Christmas gifts for his
nieces and nephews.

"What did you get the little angels?" I asked.

"Games," he replied. "I picked up the updated versions
of Clue and Monopoly."

"Updated?"

"Of course. This is the eighties, and kids today simply
couldn't relate to the way we used to play Clue and Monopoly."

"How have they been updated?" was my next question.

"Well," said Rigsby, "in Clue the rooms in the house
have been changed. The lounge is now the rec room, the
bedroom is the owner's retreat, the library becomes the
video room and what was once the ballroom is now
the spa, with sauna and whirlpool.

"The weapons are new, too. They don't have the rope, the
wrench, the lead pipe anymore. Too primitive. There's now a
choke wire, an assortment of flying Ninja weapons and a
switchblade. The revolver is a Saturday night special, and
they've thrown in a mail-order Uzi sub-machine gun."

"How about the characters?"

"Basically, they're the same, but more intriguing. As a
matter of fact, one might now use fiber evidence to prove
that Blane, the illegitimate result of an illicit affair between
Colonel Mustard and Miss Scarlett, murdered his victim by
throwing an electric vibrator into the hot tub."

"Exciting," I said. "How has Monopoly changed?"

"For starters," said Rigsby, "the tokens are no longer the
same. Instead of an old car, a top hat and a ship, there's

now a nuclear submarine, a running shoe, a miniature De-Lorean and a cruise missile.

"They've done away with the giveaway programs, too. There's a topless nightclub where Community Chest used to be.

"Baltic and Mediterranean were razed and casinos were built. If you land there on a roll of seven or eleven, you win money. If not, the house takes the two hundred dollars you just got for passing Go."

"What about railroads and utilities?"

"The government bailed out Reading Railroad, but the other three had to go the Chapter Eleven route. And watch out if you land on the Electric Company. They've just gotten a 26 percent increase on rates because of the cost overruns on the nuclear power plant they built where Free Parking used to be.

"Plant San Andreas is located there now, and if you land on it, it costs you twenty dollars to rent a radiation suit. Also, you have to pay twenty dollars for bottled water if you land on Ventnor Avenue because there was a toxic waste dump built there, and some of the waste seeped into the reservoir at Water Works next door."

"Sounds like the updated version of Monopoly is really an adventure now," I said.

"I'll say," Rigsby agreed. "I played a game with friends recently and I was doing pretty good until the other players found a minute amount of cocaine in the trunk of my DeLorean token."

"Did you have to go directly to jail?"

"No," said Rigsby. "I got out of it because they forgot to read me my Miranda rights."

Standing Up for Satan

I PHONED THE OFFICE OF SATANIC FORCES, INC., IN HELL to find out just how much the firm had to do with the recent toppling of the Reverend Jim Bakker off the evangelistic money pile.

Reverend Bakker recently resigned from his television ministry, the PTL Club, after admitting he succumbed to certain sins of the flesh, meaning he got caught fooling around in the wrong pew.

Bakker, who was bringing in a cool $129 million a year with his ministry, blamed his troubles on "satanic forces."

When the operator answered at the home office of Satanic Forces, I asked to speak to Satan himself.

"He's not in," the operator said. "He's working a book burning in Alabama. Could someone else help you?"

I explained my purpose in calling and was switched to a spokesdevil in public relations.

"Did your firm have anything to do with the recent unpleasantness involving the Reverend Jim Bakker and the PTL Club?"

"Of course not," said the spokesdevil. "We get blamed for about ninety percent of everything bad that people do and we have very little involvement with most of it."

"Do you mean," I continued, "the phrase 'the devil made me do it' is really not legitimate?"

"Listen," I was told, "the boss has enough on his hands keeping hell from going bankrupt what with the price of heating these days.

"Do you think he really has enough time to go around forcing television evangelists into illicit sexual encounters?"

"But," I interrupted, "Reverend Bakker explicitly mentioned that you were behind his fall."

"I don't know when you people finally are going to

catch on to these guys," the spokesdevil went on.

"You're making such a fuss over the insider trading scandal on Wall Street, while these television preachers are duping their viewers out of millions and millions.

"Ivan Boesky is a piker compared to the Jim Bakkers.

"Look at Oral Roberts. What a con man. He says God is going to kill him if he doesn't raise eight million.

"I ran into one of the angels changing planes the other day and he assured me God had never mentioned one word to Oral Roberts about any of that."

"You mean Oral Roberts is a fraud?"

"Not only that, he's a fruitcake. He needs to go out to Bakker's four-hundred-fifty-thousand-dollar home in Palm Springs and get some rest."

"Jim Bakker has a four-hundred-fifty-thousand-dollar home in Palm Springs?"

"With air-conditioning," said the spokesdevil, failing to hide the envy in his voice.

I said I appreciated the spokesdevil's cooperation.

"You'll be calling back soon," he said.

"When?" I asked.

"When Pat Robertson doesn't get the Republican nomination," he answered. "We're sure to get the blame for that, too."

Humor Out of This World

THE GOOD NEWS REGARDING THE RECENT SCANDALS IN-volving the television evangelists is that they have provided the opportunity for much-needed humor.

They have even revived some old material. Remember the joke about Oral Roberts starting his own record company?

It's going around again:

"Hear about Oral Roberts starting a record company?"

"No. What happened?"

"He went out of business. The hole in the middle of his records kept healing shut."

I liked the one about Jerry Falwell running into Jimmy Swaggart in an airport one day.

They began to chat and quite naturally the conversation got around to money.

"How, Brother Falwell," began Brother Swaggart, "do you decide what part of the money you get from your believers each week goes to the Lord and how much you keep for yourself?"

"Very simple," Brother Falwell explained. "Each week I take all the money my flock has sent in and put it into a large cardboard box. Then I go into my office where I have a line drawn on the floor. I throw all the money up into the air and what falls to the left of the line I give to the Lord. What falls on the right I keep."

"Very good," said Brother Swaggart. "I have a similar system of deciding how much I give the Lord and how much I keep. I also go into my office with all the money, and I also throw it up into the air and whatever the Lord catches he can keep."

I know people who are now admitting publicly they were regular watchers of the PTL Club. They didn't watch for the salvation, however. They watched for the humor.

"Jim and Tammy Faye were the best husband and wife comedy team since Burns and Allen and I miss them," a friend was saying.

"My favorite routine of theirs was when Jim and Tammy Faye both dressed up in sailor suits and Jim begged for money to pay for the water slide at Heritage Village while Tammy Faye cried. After she had cried for a few moments she looked like Soupy Sales had just hit her in the face with a mascara pie."

"I really miss both of them," my friend continued. "Watching PTL now is nothing like it used to be."

Richard Dortch and Jerry Falwell both look like they're

constipated and I can't stand to watch Jimmy Swaggart. He seems to be in such pain. Maybe he has the same problem as Dortch and Falwell.

I remain convinced humor is just as good for the soul as watching a television evangelist, and I close with the following gems currently making the rounds:

—Did you hear Oral Roberts died? The check bounced.

—How is Tammy Faye Bakker's face like a ski slope? Five inches of base, six inches of powder.

—Did you hear about the television evangelist who is a cross between Jim Bakker and Oral Roberts? If he doesn't have sex within the next two weeks, he is going to die.

Say good night, Tammy Faye.

Enough Is Enough

DURING ALL THE MESS CONCERNING THE TELEVISION evangelists, I kept wondering what's the Reverend Ike up to these days.

You remember the Reverend Ike? He is a dynamic, suave black man who preaches how God is going to make all his believers rich.

Reverend Ike, with headquarters in Boston and New York, says if you want a new car, send him a few bucks and he'll pray for you and you'll soon have your new car, compliments, I suppose, of Holy Spirit Autos.

Anyway, I now know what the Reverend Ike has been up to lately. The same old thing. Send cash, the Reverend Ike is still saying, and you will receive "health, happiness, love, success, prosperity and more money."

A friend of mine, Roy Brady, got this message in a letter he received from the Reverend Ike. Mr. Brady, who had no intention of sending the Reverend Ike the time of day, passed the letter on to me.

Here was the deal the Reverend Ike was offering Roy Brady.

In the letter, the Reverend Ike sent along what he described as a "blessed red token string."

Mr. Brady was instructed to hold the string in his hand while reading the Reverend Ike's letter.

"My eyes are filled with tears of joy as I write this letter to you," the Reverend Ike went on.

"I was working and praying for you this morning in the prayer tower and I felt in my heart you needed some extra help this month."

The Reverend Ike further instructed Mr. Brady to put his red token string into his window as soon as possible and to leave it there overnight.

Then he was to mail the string back to the Reverend Ike along with, you guessed it, a "faith donation."

The Reverend Ike said when he received the red string from Mr. Brady he would put it in the prayer tower and in no time at all Mr. Brady would get his health, happiness, love, more money, etc.

This was interesting, too.

"Do not keep this blessed red token string longer than overnight," the Reverend Ike warned.

"Get it out of your home tomorrow, no later than 8:37 P.M."

What, God closes shop at 8:37 P.M. and doesn't handle any more miracles until the next morning?

We've all had a lot of fun over the last few weeks with Jim Bakker and Tammy Faye and the boys. But do you know how many people are out there, old and ignorant and desperate, who believe the kind of bull the Reverend Ike and his ilk send out to them?

I still don't understand why the sort of letter the Reverend Ike sent to Roy Brady doesn't constitute mail fraud.

We're chasing insider stock traders while overlooking the people who are up in their prayer towers.

You want to send your money somewhere it will do some good, don't send it to these people.

Give it to your own church. Give it to the poor and homeless, give it to the hungry of the world.

Give it to the American Heart Association or the American Cancer Society or to any number of reputable charities.

When the *Charlotte Observer* began coming down heavy on Jim and Tammy Faye and the PTL Club, Jim came up with a motto around which his followers could rally against the heat of the criticism.

"Enough is enough," was that motto.

Damn right, enough is enough. It's time to run these money changers back into the black holes whence they sprang.

Going Ape over Monkey Business

A FEMALE COLUMNIST WROTE RECENTLY THAT SHE AND other women were most angry at Gary Hart because of the hurt his out-of-wedlock flings caused Hart's wife, Lee.

I can go along with that. All we had to do was look at Lee Hart's eyes as she stood steadfastly by her husband to see her agony. An observer noted in my earshot, "Hart's troubles ain't over. If he thinks the press hounded him, imagine the hell he's catching from his wife."

What I wonder, however, is why there hasn't been more said about the character and morality of Hart's partner in the recent scandal, blond and sexy Donna Rice.

You can't commit adultery by yourself. At least, I don't think you can. (It would be a good way to avoid AIDS if you could.)

It isn't that Donna Rice is some teeny-bopper airhead whom Hart charmed aboard the yacht *Monkey Business*.

The woman is twenty-nine years old, she knew full well Gary Hart was married, yet she was clearly a willing participant, whatever relationship they had, and she shouldn't get off so easily.

There used to be a word for women like Donna Rice back whenever it was I grew up. The word was "hussy," as in brazen.

It was used to describe women who were fast, loose and high-toned, and who hung around in beer joints and roadhouses, chewed excessive amounts of gum and knew all the numbers for the songs on the jukebox by heart.

I have an even better example of what a hussy was and, I suppose, still is.

My late Uncle Frank was an attorney. Once he was representing a man in a divorce case. In his summation to the jury he said:

"Ladies and gentlemen of the jury, let it be known that while my client, a brave, patriotic American, was fighting for his country on the bald hills of Korea, this woman here—his wife—was seen dancing on tabletops at Shorty's Truck Stop in Chattanooga, Tennessee, eatin' boiled eggs and drinking beer from a can."

The jury ruled for Uncle Frank's client. What else could they have done?

Jessica Hahn got off without a lot of damage, too, after it was revealed the PTL Club was paying her to keep quiet about fooling around with evangelist Jim Bakker.

Bakker lost his job and his reputation as a result, but Jessica Hahn got the money and notoriety she would have never gotten otherwise. She'll probably write a book and wind up on *Donahue*.

A reaction, or lack of reaction, toward the other halves of the Hart and Bakker tangos might be because we remain a basically sexist society.

We howl and scream at Hart and Bakker because they are—or were—powerful men. But we ignore their partners as merely a couple of broads who were nothing more than sex objects for our villains.

And where does Jim Bakker's wife, Tammy Faye, fit into all this? Now it can be told. The FBI recently ordered she take off all her makeup, and guess who they found underneath all that goo?

Jimmy Hoffa.

PEOPLE

***

Vicki's Brother Steve

V ICKI, WHO LIVES IN ATLANTA, GEORGIA, WROTE ME A
letter about her brother Steve. The letter concerned the
other side of the drunk driving issue. We pity, rightly so,
the victims of drunk driving and we work to limit their
number.

But what about those who commit what has become a
heinous crime in our society—driving drunk and killing
somebody?

We rage against them. We want them put away. We
want to see justice done.

OK, Vicki's brother Steve:

It was early October 1983. Steve got drunk at a party.
His friends urged him not to drive home. He was young
and he was foolish so he didn't listen to his friends.

He was in an accident. The accident was Steve's fault.
He escaped the accident with only minor injuries. The
other driver, also young, was killed. It would come out
later the other driver had recently received a new lease on
life. He had seemingly won a bout with cancer. Such a
waste.

According to his sister, Steve's life changed dramati-
cally after the accident. He stopped drinking and joined
Alcoholics Anonymous.

He stopped associating with his old drinking buddies.
He joined a church.

"He was consumed with guilt," wrote Vicki. "He was
determined to change his life."

Steve got married. His wife became pregnant. In early
May of this year, Steve's case came before the court.

More than fifty people wrote letters to the judge, attesting to the change in Steve's character. They asked leniency for him.

The judge gave Steve two years in prison. He is serving that sentence now. His sister has some questions she wants to ask us all:

"Many people," she wrote, "probably think two years is a short sentence for a man who has killed another. But I know Steve had already been sentenced by his own conscience to a moral prison for which there is no parole.

"The two years he is now serving are nothing more than a symbolic gesture to be carried out to placate the angry public.

"So now Steve sits in a prison cell, day after day, worrying about his crumbling business and his pregnant wife while the state does absolutely nothing that could contribute to his further rehabilitation.

"Since, in theory, one of the goals of our penal system is rehabilitation, I must ask—what is being accomplished by my brother's incarceration?

"After two months of being locked up twenty-four hours a day, Steve has finally been given a job scrubbing floors on death row. Is this how the state of Georgia rehabilitates its drunk drivers?

"I realize Steve should not have been allowed to walk away with no punishment . . . but would it not have been more therapeutic and valuable to have sentenced him to public service? Imagine the potential impact he could have on teenagers, by recounting his terrible personal tragedy.

"Steve sits, idle and bored, in his cell. His parole date is uncertain. His baby is due in November. I am struggling to maintain his business. Has justice really been served?"

It's a tough call, Vicki. You commit an atrocious act; the public wants its pound of flesh. All I can add is that if Steve's victim could forgive him, then so, perhaps, could the rest of us.

Unfortunately, he's not here.

Ottis (Smokey) Bailey

OTTIS (SMOKEY) BAILEY LOOKED ME UP ONE DAY LAST week. It had been at least a couple of years since I'd seen him.

"I been prayin' hard for you, Brother Grizzard," he said.

I said I appreciated that.

"I was even going to come see you in the hospital," he went on, "but I couldn't get a ride."

Smokey said he kept up with my recent illness through the papers.

"The Lord can shore bring you down in a hurry, can't he?" Smokey said, and I agreed wholeheartedly.

You meet some unforgettable people in my line of work. Soon after I started this column—it's hard to believe it's ten years ago—I met Smokey when I went to pick up a date at her apartment building.

Smokey was the yard man there. On the side, he was a street preacher. What was unique about his street preaching was that he did more than preach.

Each day it didn't rain he would take up a perch near one of the busiest intersections of suburban Atlanta and hand out Bibles to anyone who would take one.

We even had a send-your-Bibles-to-Smokey campaign in this column and the result was people sent in over six hundred Bibles.

"You ever give away all those Bibles?" I asked Smokey.

"Every last one of 'em," he said. "Done spread the Word all over this town."

Soon after the Bibles thing, Smokey got fired. The landlady said Smokey had been giving away Bibles instead of taking care of the apartment grounds.

143

She literally kicked him out. I found Smokey sitting on the sidewalk in front of the apartment building with all his earthly belongings, which were few.

Lord knows (I'm sure) where Smokey went after that. I would see him every couple of months or so and I would help him all I could. Like my grandfather used to say: "We never know when God is testing us. You have to help everybody you can just in case."

Smokey said he was living with some relatives now and, try as he would, he just couldn't find decent work anymore.

"Yard work just ain't around anymore," he explained. "I go by and see my regular customers and they say they done hired a landscaper and don't need me no more.

"I say, 'Listen, here, I can do yard work and landscaping, too.' They say, 'We don't need you no more.' It's a sad time when a yard man can't get no work."

"You need help, Smokey?" I asked him.

"I could use just a little," he answered.

I gave him a couple of small bills.

He smiled his toothless smile, thanked me and then he was gone.

It's a sad time when a yard man can't get no work, so you've got to help if you can.

If for no other reason, just in case.

The Legend of Willie Webb

WILLIE WEBB WAS A LEGEND AROUND THE CAMPUS OF Emory University. Thirty years' worth of Emory students and faculty and friends had known him and loved him.

They called Willie Webb "Grover" and also "The Mayor of Emory Village."

He was described to me as a little black man, five feet tall, maybe ninety pounds. For all those thirty years, he had each day occupied a bench in front of a pizza place in Emory Village and there he had imparted his wisdom and humor.

Willie Webb died the other day. The best estimate of his age was eighty-two. He had no known relatives.

Listen to Ed Green, for whom Willie once worked as a helper in Green's restaurant.

"He could see humor when everyone else around couldn't.

"The world was beautiful to him, and he was the most honest person I ever met. When he worked for me, he would sweep the parking lot. If he found any loose change, he would turn it in to me."

How Willie Webb got to the Emory area is basically a mystery, too. All anybody knew was that for years he had worked as a gardener for a local family and that a room in the family's basement was his pay. Other odd jobs put a few coins in his pockets.

According to legend, the lady of the house where he lived sent Willie out one day to dig a hole so she could plant a tree.

Sometime after dark, she remembered she hadn't told Willie to stop digging. She went outside, and Willie was still at work. He had dug a hole so deep she had to get help to pull him out.

When Willie died, some good friends tried to make certain he went out in style.

The idea was that money would be raised to pay for a decent funeral for Willie. Otherwise, he would be buried as a pauper by the county.

Friends went to a nearby funeral home and picked out a casket. They bought a new suit for Willie and costume jewelry rings for his fingers. Willie had a thing for costume jewelry.

But soon there arose a misunderstanding between the

funeral home and the friends. As someone put it, "Things got nasty."

The best I can make of it all is that after Willie was made ready for the funeral and placed in the casket, the funeral director asked for his money up front, and the friends said it would take time to arrange for full payment.

Eventually, the friends held a memorial service on campus for Willie, but the funeral home still has the body. As soon as it stops raining and somebody can dig a grave, Willie will be buried in the DeKalb County pauper's cemetery and the county will pay the funeral home two hundred fifty bucks, standard for pauper funerals.

One thing Ed Green has said: "We didn't want to see Willie buried in a pine box."

I talked to the funeral home director. He said he might just decide to bury Willie in the casket his friends picked out.

"Might as well," said the director. "He's already been in it several days and I couldn't sell it to anybody else anyway."

Touching thought, don't you think?

What Happened Christmas Eve

THERE'S SOMETHING THAT'S BEEN BOTHERING ME EVER since it happened Christmas eve:

I was driving through a very fashionable part of the city. The car was loaded with gifts and a large black dog.

I saw three men walking out of a wooded subdivision— a fancy subdivision filled with homes that cost hundreds of thousands of dollars and each of which had been decorated for the season.

The three men carried what appeared to be bedrolls.

Grizzard, the columnist, said to himself, "There's a story."

The guy in the middle did most of the talking. He said he and his two companions had left Kentucky four days earlier and that they were hitchhiking to Jacksonville, Florida, where they heard there was work.

"Been sleeping outside all the way?" I asked.

"Hasn't been too bad, except for the rain we hit outside Nashville," said the guy in the middle.

I asked the men about their families. One said he had a son somewhere, but he wasn't sure where. Another had a brother in Mississippi. The man in the middle said his wife died back in '73.

"No work in Kentucky, huh?" I asked.

The three men, their faces showing their fatigue and desperation, shook their heads.

Three men against the world on Christmas Eve in Atlanta, Georgia. Christmas has a way of tugging at the good Samaritan in most of us. Grizzard, the soft touch, reached into his pocket and pulled out $20. The guy in the middle grabbed it, and all three then God-blessed me.

"Which way to I-75 south?" the guy in the middle asked.

I told him it was three or four miles away, and I said I would take them myself but my car was filled with gifts and the black dog. They seemed to understand.

Just then a cab drove past. Darkness was closing in. Maybe if they could get to 75 quickly, I thought, they could pick up a ride toward Jacksonville before night.

I hailed the cab.

"Will you take these guys to 75 for five bucks?" I asked the cabbie.

"I don't pick up hitchhikers," the cabbie said.

"They're OK," I said.

"What's in this for you?" the cabbie went on.

"It's Christmas," I answered. "And they're hard up."

"It's worth five bucks to you to get these bums to 75?" the cabbie continued, still unbelieving.

I nodded yes.

"Is it worth ten dollars?" the cabbie said.

"I admire your Christmas spirit," I said back to him. But he had me. I was into this thing up to my ears by now.

I gave the driver the ten dollars, and the three men got inside and rode away. Later, I felt good about myself for doing a Christmas good deed.

But, I have also been wondering, would I still have stopped if there hadn't been a possible column there? Would I still have forked over thirty bucks for three strangers?

I really can't answer those questions. They come up quite often in this job.

I do know one thing, however. Regardless of my motives, I wasn't the biggest jerk in Atlanta on Christmas Eve.

That distinction goes to a certain greedy cabdriver. But I honestly hope the three men from Kentucky didn't later roll him and take my ten dollars back for themselves.

Honest I don't.

EATING OUT

✳✳✳

Cheeseburger—Hold the Mushrooms

So I'M SUPPOSED TO MEET THIS FELLOW FOR LUNCH AND he picks out the spot. It's one of those restaurants where they have a lot of houseplants, and they specialize in salads people who drink white wine and bottled water eat.

Whenever I am in a restaurant with which I am not familiar, I always order a cheeseburger. I figure no matter how bad or strange the rest of the food is, there are not a lot of ways you can louse up a cheeseburger.

The waiter comes over—his name is Keith, he tells us —and I order a cheeseburger.

My luncheon companion orders a salad called "The Californian" and a bottle of Perrier, the wimp.

A few minutes later, Keith comes back with the salad and the bottle of Perrier for my companion and the cheeseburger for me.

Right away, I know I'm in a lot of trouble. The cheeseburger, I notice, is hidden under some sort of bread that is not Official Cheeseburger Bread.

Official Cheeseburger Bread (OCB) are those buns you can buy at the grocery store that are brown on the outside and white on the inside. They are very soft and they don't have any seeds on top.

The bun surrounding my cheeseburger had seeds. I held my breath and took a bite out of my cheeseburger.

I immediately put the cheeseburger down and pulled away the top of the bun.

"ARRRRRRR!" I screamed. "There are mushrooms on my cheeseburger!"

Keith, the waiter, rushed over.

"There is something wrong?" he asked.

151

"Somebody," I roared, "has put mushrooms on my cheeseburger!"

"We always put mushrooms on our cheeseburgers," Keith insisted.

"Not on mine, you don't," was my retort.

Keith took away my cheeseburger and raked the mushrooms off. Then, and only then, would I eat it.

I vowed years ago never to eat mushrooms on anything, and I have my reasons.

In the first place, a mushroom is a fungus or a *fungi*, I'm not certain which, and it doesn't make any difference because I don't eat either one of them.

Plus, another name for mushrooms is "toadstools." That name bothers me a bit, but I can't tell you why.

Also, mushrooms are poisonous and you can die from eating them.

How do I know this Keith person isn't some kind of nut who goes around poisoning people with mushrooms because his father wouldn't let him have a pony?

I have seen mushrooms growing, too. They grow in dark, damp places. Grub worms grow in the same environment. I don't eat grub worms and I don't eat mushrooms.

"The Californian" salad, which my companion was eating, came, I noticed, with mushrooms. He ate them all.

He didn't die, which surprised me, but he did turn a little green when I told him the part about grub worms growing in the same places where mushrooms grow.

"Who knows?" I added. "One of those grub worms could have been in your salad by mistake, and you could have eaten it."

He excused himself and ran to the restroom. I wiped the grease off my mouth, and got up and walked out of the restaurant.

Another day, another day without eating mushrooms. And remind me sometime to tell you why I don't eat bean sprouts, either.

(It has to do with grasshoppers.)

Breakfast in New Orleans

NEW ORLEANS—I WENT DOWN FOR BREAKFAST FROM my room in the Fairmont Hotel. New Orleans, I might add, is still here after hosting the Super Bowl and the annual showcase for mental illness known as Mardi Gras.

I ordered what I always order for breakfast—grits, toast, bacon, two eggs medium-well and a Tab. (I realize most people start their days with coffee or orange juice, but I drink Tab, which certainly isn't as weird as some of the other stuff I do.)

As usual, I went over how to cook eggs medium-well with my waitress.

"I want the white completely done—I don't want any of it to ooze—and I want the yellow almost done, but not quite. Rather than running, I want the yellow to crawl."

I sipped on my Tab and glanced through the morning paper, awaiting my breakfast.

The big story in New Orleans was whether or not the state will legalize casino gambling. I'm all for it. Sin was invented in New Orleans. What's one more?

The waitress brought my eggs. I knew by looking at them they were prepared incorrectly. The yellow had been left on the heat far too long and it wasn't running or crawling. It was just sort of sitting there, hard as Chinese arithmetic.

"These eggs aren't what I ordered at all," I said. "The yellow is overcooked."

The waitress was very pleasant.

"I will take them back," she said.

In a very few moments she returned with my eggs and this time they were prepared perfectly.

"I'm so sorry," she said, "but I punched in your order incorrectly on the computer."

For a moment, I thought she said she had punched in my order incorrectly on a computer.

That's exactly what she said.

"You have a computer that you tell how a customer wants his eggs cooked?" I asked, shocked at the very notion of such a thing.

"We recently modernized our kitchen," the waitress replied.

How long, America, oh, how long are we going to stand for computers creeping more and more into things we hold dear, such as breakfast?

What happened to ordering breakfast, and the waitress hollering at the cook—a guy named Earl with tattoos on his arm—"Gimme a Number Three, crawling, a side of burned pig, Aunt Jemima's, roll it in dough with one of them sissy Co-colers!"

The breakfast was delicious, but that is not the point here. The point is I do not want a computer involved in any fashion whatsoever with things I eat.

Computers have caused me enough trouble, losing my hotel reservations, my airplane tickets and payments to the electric company.

"How was your service?" the cashier asked me when I went to pay my bill.

"The computer botched my egg order," I said.

"We've been having some trouble with it," she replied. "Yesterday, it was gone for an hour and a half and came back wearing a tattoo."

Hearing that made me feel a lot better.

Take Off That Tie, Pardner

TOMMY (GOOSE) MCDONNELL, A TEXAN, MOVED TO Atlanta several years ago and opened what he calls "a barbecue joint."

He started small. He found a little shack in a trendy

section of town, raised a Texas flag on top of it and called it Texas State Line Barbecue.

Tommy serves barbecue beef and pork, barbecue ribs, chili, beer in longneck, and his juke box has the late, great Ernest Tubb singing "Waltz Across Texas."

Soon after he opened, Tommy was overrun by hungry customers. He's added onto the little shack several times and he's expanded into other parts of the city.

What I like about Texas State Line is Tommy's dress code.

It's simple: Anybody who comes in wearing a tie after 8 P.M. gets it cut in half.

"This ain't no 'Twenty-one,'" says Tommy, "it's a barbecue joint."

Most men who break Tommy's dress code think it's funny when Tommy, or one of his managers, comes at them with a pair of scissors and snips their ties.

But, occasionally, he gets riffraff.

One customer called the cops after his tie was cut. The matter was settled out of court. Tommy and the irate customer went out on the deck where people were eating barbecue and drinking beer and Tommy gave him $25 for a new tie.

Another time, Tommy's manager cut off a customer's tie and the customer called Tommy at home to complain.

"Your manager cut off my tie," the man said to Tommy.

"Can't you read?" asked Tommy. "We've got signs all over the place saying that is exactly what would happen if you came in wearing a tie after eight o'clock."

"I'm never eating at your place again," said the man.

"Good," said Tommy.

The point is if other restaurants can require their customers to wear a tie, I think Tommy McDonnell has every right to insist his customers don't.

Go into a restaurant that requires a tie when you don't have one and what they will do is give you a tie a Shriner wouldn't wear to a convention in Kansas City, and you have to tie it around your neck in order to eat.

You probably looked half-way decent when you walked in. But with that ugly tie around your neck you look and feel like an idiot.

"I want my joint to have a casual atmosphere," Tommy explains. "I don't want a bunch of men sitting around in ties. It's been our policy since we started, and it's going to remain our policy."

If I ran a restaurant, I wouldn't allow anybody to wear a tie and eat my food, either.

People who wear ties are usually under a lot of stress and I wouldn't want anybody dropping dead from a heart attack or suffering a stroke in my restaurant.

I also wouldn't allow anybody in who was wearing a polyester leisure suit. He might walk past the kitchen and catch on fire.

I'd also keep out fat women in tight shorts, men in Bermuda shorts with black socks and sandals, anybody with dandruff, people who smack when they eat, people with crying babies, anybody with a tattoo, loud New Yorkers, and especially anybody who never heard of Ernest Tubb.

It's like Goose McDonnell says. To be successful in the restaurant business, you've got to keep out the riffraff.

McDonald's, Are You Listening?

FOR SOME YEARS, I HAVE WANTED TO DISCUSS SOME harsh feelings that I have concerning McDonald's, but I was always afraid nobody would agree with me. These people have sold zillions of hamburgers, so they must be doing something right.

But along comes nutritional expert-relief pitcher, Goose Gossage, who works for the San Diego Padres baseball team, which is owned by the widow of Ray Kroc, the genius behind McDonald's.

Gossage recently fell at odds with the Padres' ownership and said not only did his bosses know absolutely nothing about baseball, but they—McDonald's—also were "poisoning the world with their hamburgers."

I don't think McDonald's is out to poison anybody. You might get a little heartburn every now and then from a greasy Quarter Pounder, but you can get that in any fast food joint.

There are, however, several things that bug me about McDonald's, and now that the Goose has had his say, I feel a bit more relaxed about discussing them. Consider these points:

—Ever notice how every kid who works in McDonald's looks the same? They wear those silly-looking uniforms and those silly-looking hats and they have those knowing smiles and you've got to figure they're all going to grow up to be either chiropractors, automobile dealers or lawyers. Just what we need. More chiropractors, more automobile dealers and more lawyers.

—McDonald's foods all look like they were spit out of a computer somewhere.

I tried the new McDonald's Garden Salad the other day. It came in a little plastic box with a little plastic top and there was a little plastic fork to use to eat the salad.

Then, there were little packages of bacon bits and croutons and the salad dressing came in what resembled a tube of toothpaste.

I felt like I was eating food I had ordered by mail.

—Not only do McDonald's personnel wear silly uniforms and hats, but Ronald McDonald is a disgrace to the clowning industry. He couldn't hold Clarabell's seltzer bottle.

—The thing I dislike most about McDonald's is the suggestive selling technique of all those future chiropractors, automobile dealers and lawyers.

Ever go through the drive-in line at a McDonald's and

tell that faceless machine you want a cup of coffee?

The machine will inevitably respond by asking, "How would you like a Danish to go with your coffee?"

If I had wanted a Danish, I would have asked for a Danish.

McDonald's will also try to push their French fries off on you.

"I'll have the Quarter Pounder with cheese and a medium Coke."

"How 'bout some fries with that?"

"How 'bout sticking an Egg McMuffin up . . ." Well, you see how pushy these little brats can be.

Despite all these complaints, however, I will still go into a McDonald's occasionally just like everybody else. McDonald's is efficient. McDonald's is fast. McDonald's is ingenious in developing new food products.

There were the Chicken McNuggets. Look for the Cooked McGoose any day.

Let's Put an End to Salad Bars

AT LONG LAST, I AM GETTING SOME ASSISTANCE IN MY on-going crusade against what I consider to be a dastardly affront to the American consumer, the salad bar.

In a recent edition of *The Wall Street Journal*, there was a front-page article indicating that not only are salad bars, in my opinion, an insult to the average American eat-outer (who wants to go to the trouble and expense of dining out and then have to get up and make his or her own salad?), but they can be a health hazard.

The *Journal* points out that because salad bars usually feature a number of perishable foods and because you don't know who's been handling the food before you got up to make your salad, there is a chance you could wind up with food poisoning as a result of a visit to a salad bar.

The Journal also points out that people can sneeze on the lettuce, stick their fingers in the blue cheese dressing and drop a hair or two on the feastings as well.

There are even worse things that can happen. I quote from the *Journal*'s article: "Jack Williams, a Los Angeles County health official, was piling lettuce on his plate one day when he saw a youngster pick his nose and then use the same hand to pluck a cherry tomato and fling it back."

Grr-oss.

What happened to the salad bar in this country is what happens to a great many fads. It got out of hand.

Wendy's has a salad bar, Burger King has a salad bar and likely it won't end there. I am awaiting the day chiropractors put a salad bar in their offices.

Picking up germs at a salad bar isn't the only risk the customer takes when he or she approaches a salad bar, either.

Some restaurants do put a "sneeze shield" on their salad bars, but the problem there is you have to bend over the shield and then reach way in the back, which is where most restaurants put all the good stuff, like the cherry tomatoes.

A person could severely injure his or her back attempting to make a move only a contortionist could pull off without fear of winding up in traction. Come to think of it, perhaps chiropractors are the ones who have been behind this salad bar idea all along.

Here is what we, as Americans, should do to get rid of salad bars forever.

When you have finished giving your order and the waitress or waiter says, "Help yourself to the salad bar," you reply, "Are you out of your mind? I worked all day. My wife (or husband) worked all day. We decided to treat ourselves by going out to dinner.

"We want to sit here at this table, have a couple of drinks, and then eat dinner.

"We don't want to have to mix our own drinks. We

don't want to have to prepare our entrée, and we do not—under any circumstances—want to get up and go to the trouble of fighting the mob at the salad bar.

"We demand someone prepare our salads for us. We will tell them exactly what we want on our salads, we expect them to be brought here at our table promptly, and we expect them to be served with a smile. Understand, bean-sprout-breath?"

If everyone were that forceful, we could rid our country of salad bars and make it a much better place in which to live, raise a family and dine out.

Move quickly before one more nose-picker has the opportunity to get his hands on our tomatoes.

Middle-Eastern Chili

I TEND TO SKIP DINNER EVERY NOW AND THEN, BUT I always try to eat a tasty lunch. The problem when one travels, however, is one never knows what one is getting into when one goes into a strange restaurant. One can get stuck badly on the road.

My friend Rigsby and I were in Washington recently, and we decided to go to trendy, ethnic Georgetown for lunch.

"There's a Greek place," Rigsby pointed out.

"Let's go somewhere else," I said. "I'm afraid of terrorists in a Greek place."

We continued walking and came upon "The Georgetown Cafe." The sign outside said, SPECIAL TODAY: ROAST AND TWO VEGETABLES, $3.95.

That's what I wanted, a good American meal; meat and two vegetables. We went inside and sat down. Our waiter came over. He spoke with an accent from the Middle East someplace. I immediately was concerned.

"What are the two vegetables?" I asked him.

"Jes a minute," he said and walked behind the counter and looked at the vegetables.

"Mashed potato," he said, and then he called to the cook, "Hey, Akbar, vat is dis other vegetable?"

"Beans," said Akbar, from somewhere in the kitchen.

"Beans," the waiter said to me.

I was somewhat concerned. If a waiter has to ask the cook to identify a dish, there could be a problem with it.

I noticed that the menu just said, "roast," it didn't say roast what. I also noticed there was a picture of a camel on the menu. I don't know what roast camel tastes like, and I wasn't in the mood to try it.

However, the waiter assured me it was roast beef. So, I went with the roast, mashed potatoes and the somewhat-difficult-to-identify beans.

Rigsby, who originally is from Texas, ordered a bowl of chili.

"You're making a mistake," I cautioned him. "Why?" he asked.

"Because there are several rules to follow when ordering in an unfamiliar restaurant," I replied and quickly named several of them:

1. Never order barbecue in a place that also serves quiche.

2. Never send back food in a place where the cook is wearing a sidearm.

3. Never order anything you can't pronounce.

4. Never order chili in a place where there is a picture of a camel on the menu.

Rigsby wouldn't listen to me and ordered the chili anyway.

My meal wasn't all that bad. The reason the waiter had trouble identifying the beans is because these definitely were not indigenous to the Western Hemisphere. I should know, I've eaten all kinds of beans in my life!

The mashed potatoes were fair, and the roast beef was quite good.

When the waiter brought out Rigsby's chili, he said,

"This is Akbar's specialty, chili Middle-Eastern style."

Rigsby told me later the chili was awful, but he ate it anyway after he got a glimpse of Akbar when he walked out of the kitchen.

Another rule: Never turn down the specialty of a man who cooks while wearing a mask.

FEAR OF FLYING

***

Fear of Being Inconvenienced

I USED TO BE AFRAID TO FLY, BUT I GOT OVER ALL THAT, or most of it.

I still say a little prayer on takeoff and another during landing, and I won't fly any airlines run by Communist countries or by countries where they worship cows and allow them to wander around on the streets.

What I am really afraid of when I go to the airport these days is that I will be terribly inconvenienced.

As I have become more of a veteran air traveler, I have come to realize flying was not invented by the Wright Brothers at all.

It was originally conceived by some madman who wanted to create something to drive the human race batty. His evil ploy seems to be working.

During a recent week, I flew every day. Seven flights, seven opportunities to become angry and frustrated, seven times to ponder if we wouldn't be better off if transportation had never progressed past the Greyhound Scenicruiser.

None of the flights took off on time. On one flight we taxied out to the runway at crowded Dallas-Fort Worth headed for Las Vegas.

We had to turn around and go back, however, because some bozo who wanted to go to El Paso had gotten on the wrong plane. That cost us an hour and fifteen minutes. If I had been the pilot, I would have taken the turkey to Las Vegas and let him hitchhike to El Paso.

Another time there was some sort of mechanical problem. Lord knows, I don't want to take off in an airplane with a faulty ribbersnort or a leaky fildenstrapper, but what was supposed to be a ten-minute delay turned into two hours.

Ever sit for two hours in an airplane that won't fly? It's like being trapped in a phone booth without change.

Some other cute things happened, too. My flights were oversold a couple of times. That means they sold more tickets than they had seats and everybody who bought a ticket showed up.

What the airlines do in that case is beg passengers to give up seats in return for free tickets on future flights. That sounds like a fair deal unless you can't get off the plane for one reason or the other and have to sit through what amounts to an elongated auction.

On another flight the computer lost my reservation, and despite the fact I already had a boarding pass, I had to wait thirty minutes before I finally got a standby seat.

I know the airlines try to make flying as convenient as possible, but I wonder if they really know how difficult they can make it for passengers.

During the aforementioned two-hour delay I noticed a lady across the aisle was crying.

"Something wrong?" I asked gallantly.

"It took me a year to get up the courage to leave my boyfriend and start a new life for myself somewhere else," she sobbed. "If this thing doesn't take off soon, I'm afraid I'll chicken out and won't go."

We eventually did take off and the lady still was on the plane, but what does it say for air travel when you can't even run away from home on time.

Excuse Me, I Have a Plane to Catch

As soon as I finish writing this, I have to catch an evening flight to the West Coast. It's a Delta flight.

I probably wouldn't go if I didn't have to. The chances of another accident involving Delta so soon after that awful crash at Dallas-Fort Worth are slim, but if you read the gory details of that mishap you can understand why I'm nervous about the flight.

We've all been there before. The plane is landing in rain and thunder and lightning and is bouncing all over the skies, but we remind ourselves if flying wasn't safe, the people in the cockpit wouldn't do it as a full-time job.

But something can go wrong and something does go wrong occasionally, and when an airplane crashes, when there are explosions and fire, when there are charred bodies and dismembered bodies, the horror is magnified a thousandfold.

I will always remember a picture I saw on a private pilot's wall once. It was a picture of an airplane in a tree. The airplane had crashed headlong into the tree.

Under the picture were these words:

"Aviation itself is inherently safe, but in many ways it can be less forgiving of human error than the sea."

Human error did cause the crash in Dallas-Fort Worth. It was human error that somebody hasn't determined how to detect wind shear around an airport.

My God, we can put a man on the moon, but we can't find a way to detect wind shear, which has caused countless air tragedies?

It was human error that the plane was landing in the

violent thunderstorms in the first place. I know we have all that sophisticated radar and computers do most of the flying these days anyway, but why doesn't the FAA make a rule that says, "Thou shalt not try to land or take off in weather that has the potential to cause a plane to crash."

So my plane takes off late. So my plane is diverted to another airport to land. I can handle it. I can handle it. The usual reference to the "charred bodies" after an air disaster allows me to accept the aforementioned inconveniences.

I don't believe that "if it's your time to go, there's nothing you can do about it" nonsense.

You can buckle your seat belt when you ride in a car. That's controlling your destiny. You can refrain from driving when you are drunk or riding with a drunk who is driving.

You can put fire alarms in your house. You can get checkups for cancer. You can go to the hospital and doctors will insert a catheter into your heart to find out whether or not you are a likely candidate for a heart attack.

And you can say to the government and to the airlines you are well aware of the brilliant safety record of American passenger carriers, but that won't comfort the friends and relatives of those who died in the Air Florida plunge into the icy Potomac because of snow on the wings, of those who died in the Pan Am crash in New Orleans because of wind shear, and of those who perished in the Delta crash, again because of wind shear.

Air travel is safe, but I want it safer.

Now if you will excuse me, I have a plane to catch.

Could We Stay on the Runway?

THE DAY THE CHALLENGER EXPLODED, OVER A YEAR ago, I was involved in what now is known as a "near-miss" aboard a commercial airliner.

I was flying to Melbourne, Florida, on my way to Cape Canaveral to cover the Challenger story.

As my flight, a Delta DC-9, with news personnel from all over the country, flew directly over the launch pad from which the Challenger had lifted off, barely four hours earlier, I said to a colleague next to me:

"As nervous as flying makes me, I guess the chance of a commercial air crash is fairly unlikely this close to the Cape and this soon after the Challenger."

I often say things like that when I fly. Somebody told me it was called "positive rationalization."

We were on final approach into the Melbourne airport. We were at perhaps six hundred feet. I glanced to my left out the window and to my horror, I saw a small aircraft coming directly at me.

Later, the person sitting next to me told me I had said, "Oh my God!"

The Delta pilot swerved violently to the right to avoid a collision with the single-engine plane. A subsequent FAA investigation indicated the student pilot of the small plane had been in error and that the two planes had missed each other by only 100 feet.

Oh, my God.

Airplanes are showing an alarming tendency to run into one another or nearly miss running into one another lately.

Still, there are all the figures and all the arguments regarding how safe flying is despite the recent increases in collisions and near-misses.

But that doesn't make me any less nervous when I'm landing in a jet and I know there are student pilots and private pilots who may or may not be very good at flying an airplane, and who knows what else might be out there with which my plane could collide.

Add that to the fact the air traffic controllers are said to be short on numbers and, in some cases, experience, and the Greyhound starts looking better and better.

Statistics. You can have them, especially after I read the following, a National Transportation Safety Board report in *Aviation News* concerning a 1986 crash of a private plane in Nevada which killed a man and a woman:

"Investigators said lab tests showed the pilot's blood alcohol level was 0.18 . . . and the level of the female passenger was 0.14. In most states, drivers are considered intoxicated at a level of 0.10. . . .

"Local authorities removed the bodies from the wreckage. Investigators said local police reported that, as evidenced by the positions of the bodies and certain injuries to the pilot, the passenger was performing an act of oral sex at the moment of impact."

Oh, my God.

If You Have to Fly, Go by Bus

A WONDERFUL THING HAS HAPPENED TO ME. I RECEIVED notification in the mail recently that I have been invited to join "The Man Will Never Fly Memorial Society."

Until I received my notification, I had no idea an organization existed. But now I am fully aware, and I will be proud to help in the society's primary purpose:

The society is dedicated to debunking the myth of the Wright Brothers and subsequent, so-called man flights.

The society was born on December 6, 1959, when a group of friends had been invited to Kill Devil Hills, North Carolina, to honor Wilbur and Orville's alleged first flight on December 17, 1903, at nearby Kitty Hawk.

The night before, described by the founders as "a dark and windy night when nothing flew and even the sea gulls bounced from place to place like hoppy toads," the group began to drink heavily. The more they drank, the more they became convinced that men flying is just another cruel hoax being played on society.

The brochure that accompanied my membership offer indicated the myth of men flying has its roots all the way back to ancient times.

"First came the nonsense of Cupid flying through the air," the brochure reads. "Then, there was the nonsense of Pegasus, the winged horse.

"Next came the fabled Arabian carpet. And finally, a piece of flummery about a flying stork that dropped babies down chimneys.

"Small wonder that humankind, nourished on such nonsense, would readily believe two bicycle mechanics from Dayton, Ohio, could move through the air like winged fowl."

What, then, of the massive jets of today that are supposed to carry people from city to city at hundreds of miles an hour?

The society has an answer for that:

"Airports and airplanes are for the gullible. Little do passengers realize they are merely boarding Greyhound buses with wings.

"While on board these winged buses, passengers are given the illusion of flight when cloudlike scenery is moved past their windows by stagehands in a very expensive theatrical performance."

So that's how they do it.

I further learned the society is involved in several

worthwhile projects, one of which is a plan to build an Invisible Museum for UFO's.

Another, being tackled by the White Knuckle Chapter (Austin, Texas), is researching the octane rating of chili gas, in case someone eventually does invent the airplane.

I, of course, have long been dubious of air travel, as well as afraid of it. If you share my feelings and are interested in joining the society, write to: TMWNFMS, P.O. Drawer 1903, Kill Devil Hills, North Carolina 27948.

All you have to do is send $5 and make the pledge that is the lifeblood of the society:

"Given the choice,
I will never fly,
but given no choice,
I will never fly sober."

Train of Thought

THERE WAS A TIME IN MY LIFE—NOT TOO MANY YEARS ago—when, if I didn't drive to a place, I took the train.

The problem was the rest of the world was on a jet plane schedule, and so I had to learn to deal with my fear of flying. The way I learned to deal with it was to drink double screwdrivers before boarding the flight.

The more double screwdrivers I had, the less nervous I was on the flight. But I covered all that, of course, in my famous scientific paper entitled "The Grizzard Double-Screwdriver Theory: How I Conquered My Fear of Flying the Easy Way."

But I had this trip up to Baltimore, and who has ever been in a hurry to get to Baltimore? I decided to catch Amtrak's overnight "Crescent" from Atlanta and see what's been doing with passenger trains since I took to the skies.

The train was only fifteen minutes late leaving Atlanta.

When was the last time you were on a flight that was only fifteen minutes late?

I went to my little room in one of the sleeper cars, stowed my luggage and checked to see if my rest room was as small as I had remembered sleeper rest rooms to be. It was, and I was reminded of that wonderful love song with the touching phrase, "Passengers will please refrain from flushing toilet while the train is standing in the station, I love you."

Then, I went to the diner. One thing that has changed on Amtrak is that if you pay for a sleeper, you get complimentary meals. I had the steak. One thing that hasn't changed on Amtrak is that train food is still infinitely better than airplane food.

After dinner, I went to the club car and ordered a half bottle of red wine. It was served with a plastic cup filled with ice on the side. I certainly am not a wine expert, but I know better than to drink red wine over ice.

I unscrewed the cap to the wine bottle, sniffed the bouquet and then turned the bottle up to my lips.

"A bit arrogant," I said to the waiter after a long swallow. "But not offensive."

An older man joined an older lady in the booth next to mine. The old boy was making a move.

"I haven't had any men friends since my husband, Mr. Willoughby, died," said the lady.

"Don't worry, honey," said the man, "I'm too old to be dangerous, just still young enough not to realize it."

I went back to my sleeper somewhere between Greenville and Spartanburg, South Carolina. The elderly couple was holding hands by that time. I would have slept quite well had it not been for the fact the door to the bathroom rattled each time the train bumped, which was approximately every two seconds.

The engine broke down just out of Washington and I was two hours late arriving in Baltimore.

Still, I enjoyed the trip and I remain against any administration plans to cut the Amtrak budget.

Had the elderly pair in the club car not taken the train, neither might have realized there was yet some clickety in both their clacks.

AT THE MOVIES

✳ ✳ ✳

Don't Touch My Popcorn

NEW YORK—THIS IS INCREDIBLE, HERE I AM IN THE ENtertainment capital of the world, and I go into a movie theater on Broadway, the entertainment street of the world, and I can't buy popcorn.

There was popcorn in the movie theater. There was just nobody behind the counter to sell it.

"I would like to speak to the manager," I said to the man who had taken my ticket. "There's nobody to sell the popcorn."

"The manager's not here," said the man, "but I can tell you why there's nobody to sell the popcorn. The popcorn girl didn't show up for work."

"What's the problem with her?" I asked. "She has a new zit?" (Ever notice that all kids who work for movie theaters have terrible acne?)

"No," the ticket taker replied, "her boyfriend, Julio, lost his earring in a gangfight and she's helping him look for it."

"Why don't you sell me some popcorn?" I asked.

"No way," he answered. "The union won't let me."

I'm dying for a bag of popcorn and I have to run into Samuel Gompers.

The reason I go to movies in the first place is for the popcorn. A movie without popcorn is like a punkhead without an earring.

I always buy the largest container of popcorn available, so if the movie is long and boring, like *Amadeus*, I still have a good time eating all that popcorn.

I'm also very stingy with my popcorn. If I take a date to the movie, I always ask her politely, "Will you have some popcorn?"

Most women answer that by saying, "No, I'll just have some of yours."

I never fall for that. Nobody can eat just a little popcorn, so what happens when a woman doesn't have her own is she starts eating yours, and pretty soon, it's all gone.

I say, "Listen, you can have as much or as little popcorn as you want, but you must carry it to your seat in your own personal container. Try to get some of mine, and you'll draw back a nub."

I rarely have a second date with a woman I take to a movie, but a man must have his priorities in order.

The movie I saw sans popcorn was Rob Reiner's *Stand by Me*.

It's about four twelve-year-olds who go looking for a dead body, and nearly get eaten by a junkyard dog, run over by a train, drained dry of their blood by leeches, and sliced by bullies' switchblades. It's a comedy.

But that's about all I remember. I was too busy thinking about popcorn to pay much attention to the movie.

As I was leaving the theater, the popcorn girl finally was showing up for work with Julio and his relocated earring in tow.

"You're both a disgrace to the good name of Orville Redenbacher," I said, wishing on both the dreaded curse of large, red zits on the ends of their noses.

Harsh, perhaps, but popcorn is my life.

Today's Screen Heroes

ONE OF THE PROBLEMS FACING THE AMERICAN MALE today is his inability to emulate even in the slightest the current movie hero.

The previous generation of men had no problems doing George Raft, Jimmy Cagney, Cary Grant, or even Bogie, where all you had to do was dangle a cigarette from your mouth and react to most everything with a general unpleasantness.

And if you could swagger and win an occasional fist fight you could even remind yourself of John Wayne.

But not anymore. The box office biggies these days are men like Arnold Schwarzenegger and Sylvester Stallone, who make movies in which they singlehandedly wipe out entire civilizations.

Stallone makes movies by the number. There were *Rocky I, II, III, IV,* et cetera, and *First Blood Part II*, or was it *First Part, Blood II*? I forget. Bogie did *The African Queen*.

Schwarzenegger does things like *Conan the Barbarian* and *Commando*. Cary Grant did *Father Goose* for crying out loud.

I haven't seen all these macho men movies but I did happen to catch Schwarzenegger in *Commando* on cable the other evening. Usually, I spend my evenings in quiet meditation, but this particular evening I was feeling a bit aggressive and roguish so I clicked around the dial of my television until I found something to fit my mood.

Right away, I discovered I don't eat my red meat out of the same trough as Schwarzenegger.

I won't bore you with the plot of *Commando*, if, indeed, there was one, but among other things our muscular hero Arnold did in the movie were:

—Jump off the landing gear of a jet as it took off at two hundred miles an hour. He wasn't scratched.

—Face roughly six hundred guerrillas firing machine guns at him, never so much as getting winged.

—Kill the six hundred guerrillas firing machine guns at him, not to mention a fellow airline passenger and several thugs who had kidnapped his daughter, one of whom he dropped off a cliff, and two others he managed to impale.

I hadn't seen that calibre of impaling since the quiz show *Jousting for Dollars* went off the air.

The point is, American males always have attempted to

take on at least some of the characteristics of our screen heroes, but who can even come close to these brutish dynamos?

I could never jump off the landing gear of an airplane. The only brave thing I ever did on an airplane was attempt to go to the rest room before the captain turned off the "fasten seat belt" sign. On the way, however, a flight attendant tripped me and slamdunked me back into my seat. And when I had to collect bugs for my tenth grade biology class, I had to get my mother to stick the pins in them so they would stay in order in my cigar box. As an impaler, I'm a complete zero.

In fact, the only thing I ever did that was really megamacho was once I tried to buy a pair of undershorts like Jim Palmer models.

The sales girl snickered and showed me instead a pair of boxer shorts with owls on them, the kind Cary Grant probably wore in *Father Goose*.

Out of Africa

EVERYBODY IS GOING TO SEE THE MOVIE *OUT OF Africa*. I saw it. It's a pretty good movie. It's no *Walking Tall* or *Patton*, but for a love story with a lot of kissing and mushy talk in it, it's not bad.

There is just this one thing. The plot surrounds the fact that Robert Redford, a great white hunter in Africa, has the hots for Meryl Streep, who has somehow wound up in the same neck of the African woods as Redford, raising coffee beans for a living.

I simply can't see why Robert Redford, who probably could have anybody in Africa, would go so head-over-heels for Meryl Streep.

I realize that when one spends a great deal of one's time

out on safari, one might be attracted to a Zulu bag woman, but Meryl Streep just isn't sexy.

She's a great actress, to be sure, but so was Francis the Talking Mule.

The plain fact is that Meryl Streep does absolutely nothing for me, and if I had been Robert Redford in *Out of Africa*, I would have kept moving until I ran upon Bo Derek filming a remake of *Sheena, Queen of the Jungle*.

I admit, openly and without shame, that after I got out of the Roy Rogers, Gene Autry, Durango Kid, Hopalong Cassidy age, I began to go to movies to see pretty, sexy women.

You know who always wound my clock? Dorothy Malone, that's who.

Dorothy Malone was some kind of sexy lady. Once, I was at a Dorothy Malone movie with my friend Dudley Stamps. I forget the name of the movie, but there was this scene where Dorothy Malone was walking around with nothing on but her slip.

Dudley picked that very moment to blow up his empty popcorn bag and pop it loudly, at which time the manager of the Alamo Theater tossed both Dudley and me out.

I didn't get to see what Dorothy Malone might have taken off next, and I have never forgiven Dudley for that.

There used to be some terrific ladies in the movies. There was Gina Lollobrigida, who was in all those biblical movies. Ever notice that the best time to see a Hollywood sex queen in the slinkiest outfits was when she played some sort of pagan in a biblical movie?

I became a biblical expert by the time I was seventeen, watching Gina Lollobrigida dance for Victor Mature just before everybody got turned into a pillar of salt.

Meryl Streep isn't sexy, but Sophia Loren is. So were some of my other favorites, like Claudia Cardinale, Mamie Van Doren, Jayne Mansfield and Marilyn, of course.

Meryl Streep, if you want to know the truth, looks like this girl that was in my high school. She was tall and she wore her hair funny, and she had a big nose and played the trumpet and made all A's. Nobody liked her except the teachers.

Somehow, I get the feeling that Meryl Streep probably was a teacher's pet, too, and she maybe even played the trumpet as well.

Figures show there has been a big lag at movie box offices the past few years. I think I know why.

Instead of the sexy bombshells that once graced the silver screen, Hollywood has decided to give us former trumpet players like Meryl Streep.

The only good thing that's happened to the movies in the past twenty years, as a matter of fact, is now popcorn comes in a box instead of a bag. So if Dudley Stamps invites you to a movie now, it's safe to go.

Crocodile Dundee in the Flesh

ALEX HOPKINS DIED IN HIS HOMETOWN OF JESUP, Georgia, the other day. He was fifty-seven and he had a heart attack.

He was a burly bear of a man. The only time I ever met him, he shook my hand, grinned and then pulled a pistol out of one pocket and a pair of brass knuckles out of the other.

"I don't go nowhere without these," he said.

The man made me a little nervous.

"He acts tough, and he can be tough," somebody told me later, "but that's just the way he was raised.

"His daddy had twenty-five thousand acres of prime timberland and he knew Alex couldn't be a silkshirt and run that business.

"But deep down, ol' Alex had a heart of gold."

Characters—real ones—always have intrigued me and there aren't, it seems, many left these days.

Everybody in Jesup had an Alex Hopkins story.

—"When he got a divorce he gave his wife a thousand acres of his timberland, but he didn't tell her where it was."

—"He had a boy he wanted to be a fullback on the football team, so he made him run over plowed ground with a sack of fertilizer on his shoulders to build up his legs.

"All the boy could do after that was take little choppy steps, though, and he wound up at guard."

—"The school athletic director knew about Alex's pine trees so he asked if he would donate the poles for the lights on the baseball diamond.

"Alex said he wouldn't donate the poles but he would rassle for 'em with the athletic director—a former football player at Georgia.

"It was a big event. The athletic director wound up winning and that's how we got a lighted baseball field."

—"The IRS came to investigate Alex because he had claimed so much depreciation on his logging equipment.

"Alex disassembled his equipment into a thousand pieces. He showed all that to the IRS boys and they agreed he had a mess on his hands. What they didn't know was after they left, Alex went back out there and put all the equipment back together again and it was good as new.

"Before they left, Alex invited his visitors to lunch. He put his gun and brass knuckles on the kitchen table, pulled out his pocket knife and started slicing the ham.

"Then, he reached in the mayonnaise jar with his hand and smeared mayonnaise on everybody's bread. Then, he asked the blessing.

"'Lord,' he said, 'you know these fellers done come all the way down here to investigate me and you know I got twenty-five thousand acres and I could kill them all and hide 'em in the swamps and nobody would ever find 'em . . .'

"When Alex finished his blessing the IRS boys were halfway out of the county."

I heard that Alex had spent a year in the Savannah jail recently after getting into a fight and biting a man's ear off.

"Ol' Alex sort of reminded me of a Georgia version of Crocodile Dundee," somebody was saying.

With one obvious difference, please. Ol' Alex was damn sure real.

One *Rocky* Was Enough

WASN'T ONE *ROCKY* ENOUGH? ROCKY FIGHTS, ROCKY wins, Rocky gets the girl, Rocky is no longer just another bum from dah neighborhood.

But, no-o-o-o, there had to be a *Rocky II* and a *Rocky III* and now there is even a *Rocky IV*.

This thing is second only to AIDS in terms of harmful epidemics.

I am convinced that there is no cure for Rocky. He will be with us forever. Sequels will beget sequels and then beget them some more. *Rocky* movies will come to be known as the longest unpleasant experience in history, even longer and more unpleasant than the National Basketball Association season, pregnancy and the Punic Wars.

First, Rocky fought Apollo Creed. Then he fought Mr. T. In *Rocky IV*, he fights a Russian. And after that more of the same:

Rocky V—Rocky fights Godzilla. Rocky wins. Godzilla turns into a punch-drunk bum and runs for mayor of Philadelphia.

Rocky VI—Rocky fights former Philadelphia mayor Frank Rizzo. Mayor Godzilla fights the Philadelphia City Council.

Rocky VII—Rocky fights Tanya Tucker. Godzilla eats the Philadelphia City Council.

Rocky VIII—Rocky doesn't fight anybody but performs a country duet with Tanya Tucker.

Rocky IX—Rocky fights Willie Nelson. Godzilla runs for governor of Pennsylvania.

Rocky X—Highlights from the first nine *Rocky*'s, plus a special guest appearance by Julio Iglesias.

Rocky XI—Rocky and Julio Iglesias form a tag team and beat up Tanya Tucker and Ricky Scaggs. Godzilla wins the governorship of Pennsylvania.

Rocky XII—Rocky finds Jimmy Hoffa working in a carwash in Newark and beats hell out of him.

Rocky XIII—Rocky joins the PTL Club. Godzilla eats Jim Bakker.

Rocky XIV—Rocky fights Colonel Muammar Khadafy. Terrorists take over the PTL Club. Godzilla is nominated for president.

Rocky XV—Rocky fights David Eisenhower. Godzilla is elected president and eats Yasir Arafat.

Rocky XVI—Rocky fights Dan Rather. Godzilla eats Tip O'Neill.

Rocky XVII—PTL Club converts Khadafy, who donates the entire Libyan nation. Rocky fights Jerry Falwell.

Rocky XVIII—Jimmy Hoffa given rematch with Rocky. Jesse Jackson runs for president against Godzilla, who eats him during a debate.

Rocky XIX—Rocky fights the League of Women Voters.

Rocky XX—Godzilla eats his best friend.

Rocky XXI—Rocky fights Godzilla again, et cetera, et cetera.

AMERICA THE BEAUTIFUL

***

All Booked Up

SOMEWHERE IN THE U.S.A.—THIS BEGINS MY THIRD straight week on the road in search of publicity for a book. Some observations:

—It really doesn't matter how long it takes to fly from one place to another anymore. Once an airplane is in the air, it goes about as fast as I want it to go.

What is of consequence today, however, is how long it will take to get the plane into the air in the first place.

I've been in an airplane every day for two weeks and not a single one has taken off on time. There are traffic delays, weather delays, mechanical delays and delays where there are no explanations at all.

From the time I left my hotel, it took me eight hours to get from Chicago to Detroit. The flight itself took less than an hour.

—What we need in this country are corridor trains that go 150 miles an hour, downtown to downtown. No traffic. Shorter cab rides. Less hassle.

We won't have that, however, because it makes too much sense.

—Do you realize there is no such thing as cable TV in the city of Chicago? Something political, I presume. But where do these people get their wrestling shows without Ted Turner's Superstation?

—Until Friday, I'd never been to Minneapolis before. Now I know why.

—I asked a bellman outside a Miami hotel to call me a cab, it was late in the evening. Just then, I noticed a cab parked across the street.

"Never mind," I said to the bellman. "There's a cab across the street."

"No, no," said the bellman. "That is a fake cab. You get

inside and the driver takes off somewhere and beats you up and takes your money."

"Oh."

—At the Marquette Inn in Minneapolis the soap is blue and comes in the shape of a seashell. At the Marriott Marquis in New York, the lobby is on the eighth floor.

—When you fly on certain American Airlines flights, you get to look at a screen and see what the pilots see when they take off and land. I covered my eyes on both occasions.

—Most big hotels have what is called "Spectravision." You can watch first-run movies on your TV for a meager $5.95. I saw *Running Scared* and *Back to School* in one day in New York. Later that evening, I went to sleep during *Sexy Stewardesses*.

—Radio station WMAQ in Chicago, once one of the nation's most powerful country stations, is going all talk. Explained a DJ there, "The country music thing is all over."

—Tampa, Florida, is much too nice a town to deserve the Buccaneers.

—On a railroad bridge in Detroit somebody had spray-painted the word "Lionel."

—At the Hilton in Jacksonville, Florida, the room clerks were rude. I got even though. I took a shower and didn't put the curtain inside the tub.

Next: Los Angeles, San Francisco, Denver, Dallas, Charlotte, Nashville, Fort Worth and Baton Rouge.

That is, if I live that long.

Storing My Bag of Treks

I'M FINALLY HOME AFTER A MONTH ON THE ROAD PUSHING a book. Some notes and observations on some places I went and some people I met:

SAN FRANCISCO—I asked a woman here what it's

like to be single in a city with a huge population of gay males.

"It's terrible," she answered. "The best men you meet are married, which leaves gays and unmarried straights. Obviously gays are out and the straight guys are so arrogant, they think they're God's gift to women."

After a moment of thought, the woman added, "In San Francisco, I guess they are."

DALLAS—After several weeks of eating airplane food I was ready for some home cooking. I found it in a Dallas restaurant called The Mecca. I had country fried steak, fresh vegetables and home-made coconut pie. I asked the cook to marry me.

BATON ROUGE—A cab driver picked me up at my hotel. I said I wanted to be dropped off at a restaurant and then be picked up again an hour later and taken to the airport.

The driver said, "I'll just wait for you in the parking lot of the restaurant."

"Won't that be expensive?" I asked.

"I won't run the meter," the driver replied. "When you drive a cab in Baton Rouge, you get used to waiting and not making any money."

CHARLOTTE—This basketball-crazy town is trying to lure a professional team to the city. That news reminded me of the best line I ever heard about the National Basketball Association season, which runs from October until June.

Said Atlanta Constitution sports editor Jesse Outlar, "If the NBA had been in charge of World War II, Germany and Japan would still be in the running."

FORT WORTH—I met a man here who is planning to get married for the first time at age forty-four.

"I thought about doing something funny at the wedding, like dressing up like the Japanese did when they surrendered to MacArthur on the Missouri.

"A friend of mine reminded me of something, though. He said there are three things that do not have senses of humor, and they are brides, bureaucrats and old dogs."

NASHVILLE—I was watching the news on television here, and there was a story about airline pilots using cocaine. When the news was over, I went to the bar at the hotel and had several drinks before leaving for the airport.

LOS ANGELES—I saw the new movie hit, *The Color of Money*, starring Paul Newman and Tom Cruise here. It's a sequel to Newman's marvelous *The Hustler*. *Money* pales in comparison to *The Hustler*. In pool parlance, it scratches.

DENVER—This was in the papers. A Boulder, Colorado, man has filed suit charging he was attacked by one of the defendant's cows.

The suit says the cow is "vicious and has a dangerous propensity to charge and attack," and came at the plaintiff without provocation and rendered him unconscious.

It's nice to be back home in Georgia, although I must remind myself it was a South Georgia attack bunny rabbit that once went after the president of the United States.

Why I Like Miami

MIAMI—ONE OF THE PRIMARY REASONS I ENJOY MIAMI is there are a lot of Spanish-speaking people here and visiting gives me the opportunity to practice my mastery of Spanish, which I studied in high school and college.

The first thing I did when I landed in Miami was hail a cab. Nine out of every ten cabdrivers in Miami speak Spanish. If the Cisco Kid had lived, that's probably what he would be doing now—driving a cab in Miami.

"Buenos dias," I said to the cabdriver.

"Habla español?" he asked.

"Si," I said proudly.

The cabdriver began speaking Spanish at a rather rapid rate. The airport noise gave me momentary trouble interpreting. I figured he had asked me, "Where to?" so I told him the name of my hotel.

"El Holiday Inndo," I said.

Off we went. He said a lot of other words in Spanish I didn't quite get due to the fact I was sitting in the back seat so I said some of the things I had learned in Spanish back in school.

"El burro es un animal de Mexico," I began.

That means, "There certainly are a lot of donkeys in Mexico, aren't there?" Spanish people always like to talk about donkeys.

The driver spoke some more Spanish. Probably because of the strain of the long flight, I again couldn't quite understand him, so I said, "Beisbol es un juego de Mexico y los Estados Unidos, tambien," which means, "They play baseball in Mexico and the United States, too."

My driver, who looked a little like Fernando Valenzuela, seemed to be getting into the spirit of the conversation. He threw up his hands and made a happy sound that went "Ay-yi-yi-yi-yi!" which I seem to remember is Spanish for "I am picking the Dodgers to go all the way."

I countered with another Spanish phrase. "Páseme el pan, por favor," I said. That means, "Please pass the bread."

The driver stopped at a McDonald's and ordered me a fish sandwich.

As we drove on toward the hotel, I noticed a pretty lady walking on the sidewalk.

"La mujer," I said, "es muy bonita." That's Spanish for "My, isn't that a lovely lady."

The driver pulled over to the lady and said something to her in Spanish. There was a lot of traffic noise, and I missed what he said.

"Cien," the woman said to me. That's Spanish for "a hundred."

I wonder why she said that?

Anyway we reached "El Holiday Inndo." The bellman

took my bags to the front desk. I tipped him a quarter and said, "Gracias, mi amigo."

He threw up his hands and made the same happy sounds the cabdriver had made, "Ay-yi-yi-yi-yi!"

I never knew there were so many Dodger fans in Miami.

OTHER
THOUGHTS

***

The Salvation Army

ONE OF MY FAVORITE SOUNDS OF THE CHRISTMAS SEAson is the ringing of bells by Salvation Army people.

They normally station themselves at entrances to shopping malls and the idea is to ring the devil, if you'll pardon the expression, out of their bells in order to entice shoppers to donate money.

I interviewed one of those bell ringers for a column several years ago. I asked if he ever got tired of ringing that bell all day long.

"I hear the thing in my sleep," he said.

I bring this up to introduce the rather strange situation that developed a few days back in Rome, Georgia, a small city an hour's drive north of Atlanta.

According to a report I saw, two Salvation Army workers got themselves fired because they were unable to get shoppers to throw enough money into their pots.

I'm serious. These two ladies, Dorothy Clark and Debbie Stuart, got jobs ringing bells for the Salvation Army during the Christmas season. They were to be paid $3.65 an hour for their trouble. Mrs. Clark said she and her coworker were told they had to bring in a hundred dollars a day. When the ladies failed to meet that sum, they were axed.

Army Lieutenant Ray Tuno, their boss, "told us if our relationship with God was what it should be, we would bring in the money," said Mrs. Clark.

"But people give from the heart," Mrs. Clark went on. "What does he want us to do, hit people on the head with the bell to make them give more?"

The Salvation Army refused detailed comment on this situation. I get the feeling the Salvation Army is embarrassed, as well it should be.

It never ceases to amaze me how television preachers—and in this instance, even the Salvation Army—seem to use the threat of God when they ask for funds.

I don't know and I don't care what Dorothy Clark's and Debbie Stuart's relationships with God are, but I do know it didn't matter one red cent when the two women were out there ringing those bells.

This is something right out of the handbooks of Oral Roberts and the like. I will never forget a letter Brother Oral sent out after Jesus had come to him in a vision and told him the exact amount of money his "prayer partners" should donate to him.

The threat was there: Don't give the money, my children, and God is going to be very, very mad.

I think Mrs. Clark's comment was right on target. What did Lieutenant Tuno want them to do, hit people on the head with their bells to make them give more?

I also think I know what the answer would be to such a question:

"If you can't get their cash, give 'em a bash."

Such thoughts as these always bring tons of letters from people who ask what right I have getting involved in God's work.

I don't mess with God's work. But I also don't want a bunch of jerks using God's name to frighten people into parting with their cash.

It should be the personal conscience, and only that, which guides a person when he or she gives.

The trouble is, I'm not certain if some of the takers still have a conscience to guide them.

Curing the Common Cold

THE MEDICAL COMMUNITY HAS BEEN EXCITED RECENTLY over the discovery that a drug called interferon may be the long-awaited cure for the common cold.

I think it is only fitting, however, that we remember some of the methods that were used to battle colds in the past.

There have been some marvelous remedies—even if most of them didn't work—handed down through the years.

My mother once told me when she got a cold her mother put a lot of stuff that smelled badly into a sack and then tied the sack around her neck.

They did the same thing, incidentally, to captured prisoners in World War I to make them talk.

I, too, have developed remedies for bad colds that I have had. And just in case interferon falls on its runny nose, I thought I would mention a few of them here in case others may want to give my remedies a try.

GINGER ALE—I am convinced ginger ale can heal the sick and raise the dead. There is something about its bubbliness and sweet taste that always seems to soothe my scratchy throat and achy head.

Ginger ale will work even better if you can get somebody else to bring it to you while you are in bed. If they will talk baby talk to you while they are serving you the ginger ale, this is even better.

"Does my little tiger want some ginger ale for his coldy-woldy?" is the type of phraseology I have in mind.

SYMPATHY—I don't care what anybody says, the more sympathy you get when you've got a cold, the faster you will recover.

It probably won't do you any good to call any of your friends looking for sympathy, so the best place to find it is to call your mother.

If she says something like: "Does my little tiger have a coldy-woldy?" you can expect to be up and around in no time.

MOANING AND WHINING—These have been two of my favorite cold remedies. What you do is get into the fetal position and moan or whine.

A moan and a whine are different. When you moan you make low grunting sounds like "Oooooooh, my God." When you whine, you make sounds like a poodle dog yapping for its dinner. I don't know how to spell what a poodle dog sounds like when it is yapping for its dinner, but you get the idea.

Even if nobody is around to hear you moaning and whining, it will still help your cold. If somebody is there to hear, however, that's a lot better.

OLD BLACK AND WHITE MOVIES—Nothing helps a cold more than lying in bed drinking ginger ale, getting sympathy from somebody while you are moaning and whining, and watching an old black and white movie on television.

If Jimmy Stewart, Barbara Stanwyck, Alan Ladd, Victor Mature or Yvonne DeCarlo is in the movie you probably will be well by the next morning. If Ronald Reagan is in the movie, however, you can be flat on your back for weeks.

CHICKEN SOUP—This, of course, is the all-time homemade remedy for the common cold.

I really don't know if chicken soup works on a cold, but in the immortal words of my mother, who was kind enough to feed me chicken soup when I had a cold rather than tying smelling bags around my neck, "Have you ever heard a hen sneeze?"

Think about it.

Spitting Images

Picture me riding with this lady in my car. We are at a stoplight. A man pulls up next to us in a truck.

The man opens the door and proceeds to spit a large dollop of tobacco juice onto the street. The lady in my car is horrified.

"Gross!" she exclaimed. "How could anyone do that in public?"

I realized the lady was not aware of the major problem involved with chewing or dipping a tobacco product. Although I do not indulge in either myself, I have known a great many chewers and dippers, and I realize that having to spit quite often is one of the major side effects of such practices.

"He probably just forgot his spit cup," I said to the lady.

"Spit cup?" she asked. "Gross! Let's drop the subject. I'm getting sick to my stomach."

I could very well have argued with the lady and pointed out that people were chewing and dipping and spitting into various containers long before she graced the planet and that containers of spit actually have a place in the oral history of our country.

Was it not John Nance Garner, the Texan, who once compared the job of vice president of the United States to, in his own words, "a warm bucket of spit?"

I'm not certain when spitting developed such a bad image in this country, but it probably was about the same time people started putting mushrooms on cheeseburgers.

I used to spit a lot myself, even though I didn't use tobacco. A friend and I used to go to a bridge near my house and spit into the creek below.

The game was to see who could spit closest to a floating

leaf or stick. Some kids had Little League. We had bridge-spitting.

Both grandparents on my mother's side dipped snuff and they spat a lot. In fact, my grandfather could spit at a fly six feet away and get it every time. Who needed a fly swatter when my grandfather had a little Bruton's under his gum?

Chewing and dipping have made a slight comeback recently, and that is because people most likely are substituting smokeless tobacco for their cigarettes.

I have a friend who chews tobacco—Beechnut. I asked him about the social ramifications of his pastime.

"It does come in handy always to have a spit cup," he explained. "Otherwise, you are either going to have to swallow the spit or just let it go wherever, like the fellow in the truck.

"Of course, those of us who are concerned about what others think of us usually put some tissue in the bottom of our spit cups. That way, if we accidentally turn them over, the tissue will have soaked up the spit and it won't run all over everything and everybody."

I asked him if his wife had learned to live with his chewing and his spit cups. I swear I didn't know about the divorce until that very moment.

I realize spitting can be disgusting to others, but I still don't think it's the worst thing in the world somebody can do.

It's like on a New York subway train. You can get heavily fined if you spit. On the other hand, you may throw up for nothing.

My Sockless Stance

A FEW EVENINGS AGO I HAPPENED TO BE AT A FANCY dinner party. I call any dinner party where you have to say "Excuse me" when you burp fancy.

As we were being served coffee after the meal, I crossed my legs to get more comfortable. The hostess noticed I wasn't wearing any socks. She was aghast.

"You aren't wearing any socks!" she aghasted, if that is a word. If it's not, then she exclaimed.

"Socks, my good woman," I began, "are among the most useless things on earth, just behind flyswatters and just ahead of ties. I wear socks only when they are absolutely necessary, and that occurs only when the temperature is such that if I go sockless there is a chance my feet may become frostbitten."

Wearing no socks has become a sort of trademark of mine, and most people think I go sockless in order to make the statement I am—how do you say it?—"laid back."

This is simply not true. My sockless stance actually has its roots in my formative years growing up in Moreland. Since most of the children in my school were from a rural background, it was considered quite unnecessary to wear shoes, much less socks, until the first good frost.

I was in high school when I developed my disdain for socks. Having never taken that much heed of fashion trends, I was in the 11th grade and shaving thrice weekly before I got the word white socks were not considered appropriate footwear for any event that did not involve athletic endeavor.

I was at a dance at the National Guard Armory doing the "mashed potatoes" with Kathy Sue Loudermilk when somebody noticed I was wearing white socks with my loafers.

Word spread quickly. I eventually was hooted from the floor because of my white socks, and Kathy Sue was so embarrassed she locked herself in the restroom and would not come out until she was certain I had left the premises.

This night of mockery and shame had a profound effect on me. Since I never could be sure when I might choose the wrong socks again, I simply quit wearing them in nonblizzard conditions.

Think of the money I have saved over the years by not having to buy socks. Do you realize what men's socks cost today? They are outrageously overpriced.

I remain convinced that if the Lord had wanted men to wear socks, he never would have allowed Christian Dior to sell them for ten bucks a pair.

Some may ask, do you wear socks at such occasions as weddings and funerals? Weddings, never. Not even my own, after the first couple, when getting married sort of became a casual routine for me.

Funerals, it's a tossup. It sort of depends on how well I knew the departed. I wore socks to my grandmother's funeral, for instance, but I didn't wear any to my bookie's, who died in a freak hunting accident in front of his favorite Italian restaurant.

As to whether or not I will wear socks to my own funeral, I'm not sure. It depends on the weather.

Dinner at the White House

WASHINGTON—I'M NOT CERTAIN HOW IT CAME TO PASS that I was invited to a White House state dinner in honor of, as it said on the invitation, the visit of His Excellency, The Prime Minister of India, and Mrs. Gandhi.

I don't know anything about India except they allow

cows to wander around in the street over there because they think cows are sacred. I don't have anything against cows, but I'm glad we don't think they are sacred over here, because if we did there wouldn't be any such thing as a bacon cheeseburger.

When I responded to the social secretary of the White House to accept the invitation, I asked how long the dinner would last.

"I'm not sure," she said. "Why?"

"Because if I don't have my tux back to the rental place by eleven, I'll have to pay extra," I explained.

She laughed, nervously.

I had a great time at the White House. When you walk into the Gold Room for dinner, you have to pass through a foyer where the press and the photographers are located.

I walked in behind Loretta Young, the actress, who looked darn good for a woman three hundred years old, and Dr. Henry Kissinger and his wife, who resembles a cornstalk and smoked one cigarette after the other despite the fact ashtrays are at a premium at the White House. Oh well, there's always the floor.

The press asked Loretta Young and Dr. Kissinger a lot of questions, and all the photographers snapped pictures of their entry into the dinner.

Nobody took my picture when I was announced, but a lady from the *Washington Post* did ask if this was my first trip to the White House.

"Surely, you jest," was my reply. "The last time I was here, we all sat in the back yard and drank beer and listened to Willie Nelson."

Say what you want to about Jimmy Carter, but the man knew how to throw a party at the White House.

Know who provided the after-dinner entertainment at Reagan's party for Prime Minister Gandhi? Some bald-headed guy who played the cello, that's who. He had a foreign name President Reagan had trouble pronouncing when he introduced the man to the dinner guests.

Cello players, I decided, are a lot like alligators. You've seen one, you've seen 'em all.

The food? We had Crab and Cucumber Mousse, Supreme of Cornish Hen, Wild Rice with Toasted Walnuts and Baby Zucchini. We had Bibb Lettuce with Garden Chives and Grape Cheese, and we had Chocolate Boxes with Fruit Sorbets and Peach Champagne sauce.

Our wines were Bacigalupi Chardonnay (1983), Saintsbury Garnet (1983) and Schramsberg DemiSec, which I found assertive, but not offensive. My only complaints with the meal were that there were no soda crackers to eat with the salad, and I am foursquare against the slaughter of baby zucchinis.

I got to shake hands with the president. He is a nice man, but he is shorter than I thought he was. I chatted with Mrs. Reagan, who has a very nice smile in person. I met Maureen Reagan, who needs to lose a few pounds, and I danced with a dress designer from New York who spoke with a British accent despite the fact she was from Missouri.

When the party was over, I went back to my hotel and ordered a bacon cheeseburger from room service and ate it while sitting in my underdrawers.

Holy cow, I thought to myself, what a perfect way to end a storybook evening.

Bing Won't Be Home...

I WENT OUT TO BUY SOME CHRISTMAS MUSIC. WHAT I like to do during Christmas is build a fire, sit by it and listen to, as the radio announcers say, songs of the season.

What I really wanted was Bing Crosby. Christmas comes and I normally think of Bing Crosby singing "White Christmas" and "I'll Be Home for Christmas."

I went into one of those stores that carry albums and tapes.

One of the sales clerks, a girl perhaps eleven years old, waited on me.

"I'd like to see some Christmas tapes," I said.

"Any particular artist?" she asked.

"Yes, I'd like to see some Bing Crosby."

"You mean Crosby, Stills and Nash?"

"No," I continued. "Bing Crosby. You know, Hope's pal. *The Bells of Saint Mary's* and all that."

"I'm afraid we don't carry Ben Crosby," the girl said.

"Not 'Ben,'" I tried to explain. "It's 'Bing.' He smoked a pipe and . . ."

"I'll get my supervisor," said the clerk.

That's more like it, I thought. At least now I could deal with an adult.

"There is a problem, sir?" asked the supervisor. He might have been nineteen.

"No problem. I just want to buy a couple of Bing Crosby Christmas tapes. My dog ate the old ones."

"Would this Crisby . . ."

"Crosby."

"I'm sorry. Would this Crosby be Rock, Country and Western or Rhythm and Blues?"

"I can't believe this," I said. "Bing Crosby was one of the greatest singers who ever lived. His Christmas music is legendary. You mean to say you've never heard of Bing Crosby?"

"He must have been a little before my time," the supervisor explained. "We do have a rather extensive list of Christmas albums and tapes by other artists, however. Would you like to see some of them?"

"Sure," I said. "How about Perry Como? Do you have any Perry Como?"

"No, but we do have Nasty Ned and His Nine Nasty Nose Pickers and their Christmas album, *Rock Around the Christmas Tree Until You Throw Up*."

"No, thanks. How about Andy Williams?"

"I don't think we have that, either. But we do have Stark Nekkid and the Car Thieves and their latest, *Santa Got Caught in my Chimney and the Bats Ate Him*."

"Johnny Mathis?"

"Nope."

"Roger Whittaker?"

"Afraid not."

"Robert Goulet?"

"Never heard of him."

"Steve Lawrence and Eydie Gorme?"

"Aren't they on *Hart to Hart*?"

"Forget it," I finally said. "Just show me where you keep all your Christmas music and I'll make a decision."

I wound up buying *The Chipmunks' Christmas*.

They aren't Bing Crosby, but for small, burrowing animals, they don't sing half bad.

Other People Who Should Be Drug Tested

SOMETHING'S BEEN BOTHERING ME ABOUT THE IDEA OF giving professional and collegiate athletes tests to determine whether or not they are using drugs.

Don't misunderstand me. I pay good money to watch my favorite teams play, and I would prefer the participants in the game be of clear head.

My favorite baseball team, the Atlanta Braves, have enough trouble winning games because of their lack of talent. Throw a few druggies into the picture and they might decide to send the entire franchise down to Triple A.

My concern, however, is this: We're so worried about athletes not using drugs, we're forgetting others who are of much more importance than some kid who can bounce a ball.

I have compiled a list, as a matter of fact. If I had to, I could live with the entire National Basketball Association in dopeland. But not the following:

1. Airline pilots: I want to be assured that all pilots of all airlines, big and small, are not taking drugs. Some of that stuff can cause one to hallucinate. I don't want my pilot seeing a runway that isn't there.

2. Surgeons: Would you really care if the entire backfield at your alma mater was on drugs if you found out the guy who was going to remove your gallbladder next week kept a little cocaine in his locker to help him relax and get to those hard-to-reach places? Get all the surgeons clean. We can worry about the Yankee bullpen later.

3. Dentists: Same as above. This man is up to his elbows in my mouth with a sharp instrument in his hand, and I want to be certain he isn't plugged into the nitrous oxide tank with me.

4. The guys in the silo with the nuclear button:

"Hey, Harv, what are these little buttons for? I forget."

"Don't know, Sam. Give me another pull on that joint and then push one and find out."

Don't even allow these people to have a strong mouthwash.

5. Joan Rivers: She already talks at Mach I. Shoot her up and she'd probably talk so fast she would suck up all the oxygen on the planet.

6. Barbers: "Heeeey, look at that. Took that ear right off, didn't I?"

7. Hunters: Imagine the first day of deer season, and Lonnie Bob's out in the woods with his gun and he's high on something a little stronger than his Red Man chew:

"OK, if you say so, it wasn't my horse you shot. It was a deer. Now, if you'll just put that gun down and let me get my saddle off, he's all yours."

8. Fishermen: They lie enough as it is.

"Catch any fish?"

"Caught the Loch Ness monster, man."

"What did you do with it?"

"Threw it back, man."

"Why?"

"I didn't want to have to clean that sucker, man."

You're probably wondering why I didn't mention politicians here. The reason I didn't is because politicians are a lot like wild beasts. Drugged, they're a lot less dangerous.

Earthquakes Frighten Me

LOS ANGELES—AS SOON I STEPPED OFF THE PLANE HERE in Los Angeles, I bought myself a newspaper. A word jumped off the front page at me. That word was "earthquake."

There are lots of words that frighten me. "War" is one. "Snake" is another. And I've never been overly fond of "alimony" either.

But "earthquake": as in the ground opens and swallows you up.

The paper said that only one day before I arrived here, a quake registering 5.9 on the Richter scale had tossed southern California hither and thither. There was a lot of damage, a few injuries, but nobody had been killed.

What really caught my attention, however, was the suggestion that continuing shock waves from the original quake might set off a few more in the next couple of days, the exact length of my visit.

I went directly back to the Delta counter to book myself the next available return flight to Atlanta, where there never has been a recorded earthquake.

My traveling companion tackled me, however, and took away my wallet and credit cards. Quite reluctantly I ventured on to my hotel.

I was assigned a room on the eleventh floor.

"Do you have anything lower?" I asked.

"What do you have in mind?" asked the clerk.

"A very secure metal vault in the basement," I said.

The clerk laughed. "You're afraid of another earthquake," he said. "All our out-of-town guests are the same. But don't worry. A 5.9 on the Richter scale is nothing."

For years scientists have been warning that there definitely is going to be a major earthquake in southern California, a catastrophic earthquake that could cause the entire area to fall off into the Pacific Ocean. Scientists further say it could come at any time.

What is amazing, however, is the locals seem unconcerned.

"That last quake came at two in the morning," a native was telling me. "I slept right through it."

"I worry more about the smog or getting killed on the freeway than I do about an earthquake," said another.

Me, I've been the proverbial cat in a room full of rocking chairs for nearly forty-eight hours.

Everywhere I walked, I walked very slowly, making sure each step was on terra firma that wasn't doing the boogaloo before I took another.

I've been very careful to notify waiters not to fill my coffee cup completely full. In case of a quake, I don't want to spill hot coffee on myself.

Whenever I've waited on the street for a cab, I've tied myself to the nearest light post with my belt in case a tremor suddenly came and the flat horizon was suddenly downhill.

So far, so good. Southern California is still basically intact and so am I, and in just a few more hours I will be out of here.

If I make it, thanks Lord. If I don't, tell my mother I remembered to brush every day and I never wore dirty underwear unless it was absolutely necessary.

"Don't worry," the hotel clerk had said. "A 5.9 on the Richter scale is nothing."

It's not the Richter scale that bothers me. It's Richter mortis.

There's No Accounting About Taxes

I DROPPED BY TO SEE MY ACCOUNTANT, WILLARD "THE Shark" Houdini. He was in a most jocular mood.

"I'm celebrating," he said.

"Let me guess," I said. "You finally had a client survive an IRS audit?"

"Very funny," he replied. "What I am celebrating is the new tax bill. Have some champagne?"

I declined. Never accept an offer of champagne from an accountant wearing a skyblue leisure suit. That's one of the first things you learn in Economics 101.

"Pardon my ignorance, but I thought accountants were going to lose business because of the new tax bill, which was supposed to simplify how we do our taxes."

"Are you kidding me?" said Willard. "Have you ever known anything to come out of Washington that was simple?"

He had a point.

"Listen," he went on, "this new tax deal is the best thing to happen to accountants and lawyers and financial consultants since the three martini lunch.

"Nobody has any idea how this new tax thing is going to work or how they are supposed to find the loopholes in it."

"But," I interrupted, "I thought the new tax law was supposed to do away with loopholes."

"Do away with loopholes? That would be un-American."

I was confused.

"Let me tell you what all this is really about," said Willard.

"In the first place, it's an election year and nobody is going to vote against tax reform that allegedly will lower taxes. So here's what's going to happen: Real estate tax shelters, where rich people hid their money, will become obsolete, and the tax liability for people who make a lot of money will increase and big companies will owe a lot more taxes, too."

"That's what I thought," I said.

"You don't understand," said Willard.

"Rich people who can afford the fees will go to see their accountants or financial consultants and lawyers to see what they can do about lowering their tax liability and some smart cookies will find a way.

"As far as the big companies are concerned they simply will pass along whatever increase they have to pay to their customers."

"But aren't the poor people getting a tax break?" I asked.

"Sure," said Willard, "but don't forget this. Not only will prices for goods go up, but there will be a slowdown in construction of, say, new apartments, so apartment owners will be able to go up on their rents and the poor will still get the shaft."

"Isn't there something that can be done about such an inequity?" I asked.

"Of course," explained Willard. "This time next year there will have been so much griping and complaining and lobbying that the big companies will get their tax breaks back, and well-off individuals will be back in the tax-shelter game. It's just a matter of time."

"And the poor?"

"They aren't my problem," said the Shark, guzzling another swig of champagne.

Don't Try to Convert Me, Please

RELIGIOUS FREEDOM IS A WONDERFUL THING. THE search for it and the need for it is what brought about this country in the first place.

If we didn't have religious freedom, then we might have somebody saying, "Worship the way we tell you to, or we'll kill you." Tragically, this has been said often throughout history.

I have nothing against any religion. If somebody doesn't believe exactly as I believe, that is fine with me. If more people thought like that, then the world likely would be a much safer place in which to live.

I would, however, like to address one particular religious group and ask them a favor.

I would like to tell the Jehovah's Witnesses once and for all that I am not interested in discussing their beliefs with them.

I was never interested before, I am not interested now, and I will not be interested in the future.

As I stated earlier, if you want to be a Jehovah's Witness, that's your business. But, please, take me off your list of possible converts, and don't come to my house anymore.

My grandfather had a lot of trouble with Jehovah's Witnesses. He referred to himself as a "foot-washing Baptist," but he quit going to church when he discovered ministers were using notes while delivering their sermons.

He believed, as was his right, ministers should be guided by the Lord while they are addressing their flock and the use of notes was, in his mind, probably the work of the devil.

Jehovah's Witness missionaries began to call on my grandfather. They wanted to convert him and sell him their pamphlets.

My grandfather was a kind, patient man, but not one to be riled. After he had politely told about eight million Jehovah's Witness missionaries to please not knock on his door anymore he had all he could stand.

As soon as he saw the next group of missionaries pull into his yard, he got his shotgun and explained to the visitors he preferred they be off his property in three seconds. They complied with his wishes in two.

I was working at my house the other day. I heard my dog barking. My dog, Catfish, the black Lab, always barks when someone drives into my driveway.

I looked out my window and saw two women standing at the bottom of the steps. Catfish's barking, with an occasional growl thrown in, had stopped the women dead in their tracks.

I walked out and asked their business.

"We're Jehovah's Witnesses," one of the women said. "We would like to talk to you."

"I'm sorry," I replied, "but this black dog is trained to eat Jehovah's Witnesses. Got two last week."

The ladies left, Catfish went back to his nap, and I went back to my work.

Again, I have nothing against Jehovah's Witnesses except they bugged my grandfather, and they've hit on me a number of times, as well, and I'm very happy with the religious beliefs I happen to have at this point in my life, thank you, and I don't want my mind changed. And that is my right.

Catfish, incidentally, feels the same way.

In the Public Eye— and Irritating It

I OFTEN WONDER WHY ANYBODY WOULD WANT TO RUN for political office. It's expensive, it's tiring, and you have to kiss a lot of fat babies, and fat babies have a habit of drooling on you when you try to kiss them.

And after you're elected, although you do have a good opportunity to become wealthy in some instances, you still have to wear a tie to work every day, people write nasty letters about you in the newspapers, and if your kid gets arrested for shoplifting you have to deny you even know the little devil or face losing when you run for reelection.

All that was bad enough, but in the recent national elections, we had a new twist known as negative advertising.

This is where you pay an advertising firm two or three million dollars to invent television and radio commercials saying your opponent has bad breath, sleeps in his underwear and doesn't love the Lord.

I happened to be doing a great deal of traveling during the final weeks of the campaign, and after seeing negative commercial after negative commercial, I became concerned that every candidate running was some sort of dishonest mudbrain.

Began one: "Do you really want a man like Harvey Snucklehouser representing you in Washington? He cheats on his income tax, doesn't put the shower curtain inside the tub when he bathes in hotel rooms, his mother wears combat boots and he pulled for the Mets in the World Series."

Another said: "How could anybody vote for Bernice (Dingbat) Flournoy? She's so stupid she thinks Beirut was a famous baseball player, she smells like a goat herder, probably is a Communist and has fat thighs."

In Georgia, incumbent Republican Senator Mack Mattingly basically stayed out of his campaign with the exception of buying commercials that said his opponent, Democrat Wyche Fowler, hardly ever bothered to appear for votes during his term as U.S. representative.

Fowler got even, however; he beat Mattingly, who won't be making *any* appearances in the Senate anymore.

I have a friend who once ran for a local county post. He lost.

"It was the worst experience I ever had," he said. "Every time I told a lie, they caught me, and every time I told the truth, nobody would believe me."

There are lots of better ways to abuse oneself than going through the expense, turmoil and humiliation of running for and holding political office.

You could open a meat market in Ralph Nader's neighborhood, get a job as Frank Sinatra's press agent, or become a newspaper columnist and say you think television evangelists are a bunch of crooks.

I once asked a man who was running for Congress just why on earth he would want to put himself through such an ordeal and have people say bad things about him and be mistrustful of him.

"Well," he replied, "I was already a lawyer."

In my mind, that's still not reason enough.

At the Root of Dental Dismay

I SPENT AN AFTERNOON IN MY DENTIST'S OFFICE LAST week. My dentist is a nice man, and I feel he is sincere when he says, "Gee, I'm sorry," after he goes for one of my bicuspids with his drill and misses and nearly takes off one of my ears.

"Never did have very good aim," he further apologizes as I make my way back to the chair from the ceiling.

I don't have anything personal against dentists, unlike author Robert L. Steed, who once asked, "Why are dentists free men?"

Dentists mean well, I am certain, and without them many of us would be down to nothing more than our gums by now.

It's just that the dental profession, were it to stop and think for a moment, could do a great deal to ease the discomfort and fear many of their patients feel.

Let's start at the very beginning. I go to my dentist's office, and while in the waiting room, if I can stop trembling long enough, I attempt to read one of the magazines my dentist provides his patients.

Last week I picked up a copy of *Sports Illustrated*. It was an issue from 1979. This caused me to think: If this guy is too cheap to pop for any new magazines in his waiting room, he's probably not going to waste any money on modern dental equipment either.

Let's say he is going to extract one of my wisdom teeth on this particular visit. I expect one of two things:

Either he's going to tie one end of a string around my tooth and the other around the doorknob of his office door, and wait for his insurance salesman to walk in. Or, he's going to put one hand in my mouth and reach the other toward his assistant and say the dreaded word, "Pliers."

Speaking of dreaded words, people wouldn't be nearly as afraid of the dentists if dentists would change the names of some of the terms they use.

Let's take the word "drill," for instance. That's not a happy word. That's a scary word. It should be used in the context of oil wells and military exercises and not in relation to my mouth.

Pulp is another dental term I don't like, as in "Sorry, but I just drilled all the way down into your pulp."

Pulp is where your teeth keep all their nerves and other innards. When I hear the word pulp it reminds me of a movie I saw once where Sir Laurence Olivier played a former Nazi dentist, and he drilled into the pulp of Dustin Hoffman on purpose in order to get him to talk.

The very thought of that makes me want to give away military secrets right and left even if I have to make them up.

The worst dental phrase of them all is "root canal." Who thought of such a horrid, frightening term? Probably a Nazi. But dentists, including my own, still use it.

"Looks like you're going to need a root canal here," my dentist said last week.

"The attack is coming in early June on the Normandy coast," I replied.

"I beg your pardon?" said my dentist.

You can't blame me for trying.

If laughter is the best medicine, then
LEWIS GRIZZARD
is the cure.

*

Published by Ballantine Books.
Available in your local bookstore.